KU-486-935

CONTENTS

California Condor

Red-thighed Falconet

INTRODUCTION

The birds of prey make up the order Falconiformes. It includes the buzzards, eagles, falcons, harriers, hawks, and the vultures. There are about 290 different kinds of species in all. Some authorities recognize only about 270, because it is difficult to decide whether two closely related types, separated perhaps by an ocean or a desert, should be considered as forms of the same species or whether they have really evolved into truly different species.

The 130 or so species of owls, which make up the order Strigiformes, are all more closely related to each other than are the birds of prey. Owls also vary greatly in size, the tiny Elf Owl being the size of a pygmy falcon whereas the Great Eagle Owl is nearly as large as a Golden Eagle.

People give the name eagle to many large birds of prey which are not necessarily related to each other. The sea eagles are really very large kites and many other so-called eagles are

Great Eagle Owl

Elf Owl

related to buzzards or harriers. Several of the birds known as true eagles are actually quite small.

The American vultures may not be related to other birds of prey at all but may simply be scavenging birds which have evolved on similar lines to the Old World vultures although coming from quite different stock.

Two other birds, the Secretary Bird and the fish-eating Osprey, have puzzled ornithologists for centuries, but they probably are related to the rest of the birds of prey. Of the rest, the falcons are the most distinct and have evolved a number of anatomical differences which separate them from the rest of the order.

Most people think of birds of prey as eaters of warm-blooded animals, but this is not always so. Some eat a wide variety of cold-blooded animals and some are even partly vegetarian.

Some of the birds of prey are very small, some pygmy falcons being hardly larger than a sparrow. But they are more of a bird of prey than is the condor with its ten-foot wing span as they can kill birds much larger than themselves, even twice their size.

5

SPECIAL CHARACTERISTICS

Wings and Tails

A bird of prey uses its wings to reach its food. It may be a case of finding a dead animal in a large expanse of open country or of catching another bird flying at 80 miles an hour. Perhaps it must catch flying ants or cling to a wasp's nest and feed on the insects inside.

Finding such a wide variety of foods must involve very different activities. Different types of birds of prey have evolved various types of wings, according to the type of hunting they specialize in. The ten large primary feathers which form the wing tip and are responsible mainly for the speed of a bird may be long or short. The secondary feathers at the rear of the wing are responsible for lift, and they too may vary in length and in number, according to the length of the bird's forearm.

A bird such as a vulture which looks for dead animals will often need to fly perhaps 200 or more miles in a day. Flying, especially flapping flight, can consume a great deal of energy. For this reason, vultures have developed very long, broad

Lanner Falcon

Himalayan Griffon

wings to enable them to soar easily and then to glide for great distances with very little flapping. The big disadvantage of large wings is that they make taking off and landing cumbersome, but since most vultures do not have to catch their food, the advantages outweigh the disadvantages. In contrast to their huge wings, vultures have small tails. The tail, which in birds of prey is composed of twelve or occasionally fourteen strong feathers, acts as a rudder. Since vultures seldom need to turn quickly, they need only a small tail.

Large eagles (which often eat carrion) have rather shorter, narrower wings than do vultures. They also have a much larger, stronger tail, and these adaptations enable them to land and turn quickly when seizing prey moving on the ground.

Certain birds of prey, such as some of the kites, have long narrow wings and yet are accomplished at soaring and gliding. They are, however, very light: no really strong, heavy bird can soar on narrow wings except in ideal weather conditions.

Certain birds of prey possess fairly long wings and are lightly built but very seldom soar. For instance, the harriers, which glide low over open country and marshland and catch prey by surprise, proceed by a few flaps followed by a glide.

Shikra

Montagu's Harrier

Hawk Owl

Many birds of prey, from tiny hawks to the largest eagles, have become hunters in forests and well-wooded country and are adapted for catching the various birds and mammals that live there. They have evolved short, broad wings and long tails. With this combination they are able to fly rapidly among the trees and to turn very sharply as the prey – it may be anything from a small bird (in the case of a hawk) to a monkey (in the case of a large eagle) – tries to reach cover.

Most of the falcons have narrow wings, the heavier ones having wings broader at the base which let them soar effectively. Long, narrow-tipped wings enable a bird to fly very quickly and most falcons catch their prey by pursuit. When hunting other birds, some falcons soar above their prey and then dive from the height gained, using the extra diving speed to overtake their victims. This is called ''stooping'' and the Peregrine Falcon is particularly fond of this method of hunting, stooping on its victims at an incredible speed, often at an almost vertical angle and knocking them out of the sky with its talons.

As many birds of prey are frequently seen only when they are soaring high in the sky, identification can often be extremely difficult. The precise shape and pattern of the wing is therefore important in distinguishing between species, and so are the length, shape and pattern of the tail. Slight variations in underwing markings and wing-shape enable the experienced observer to identify many species which to the beginner look identical to one another. The angle at which the wings are held may also help to identify a particular bird of prey or at least narrow down the possibilities.

Little Owl

Short-eared Owl

Owls' wings are much less variable in shape than are those of the other birds of prey. No owl searches for carrion from a great height (as of course this would be impractical in the dark), so none has very long, broad wings.

Many owls, such as barn owls and marsh owls, hunt over open country rather in the way that harriers do and have developed long, narrow wings similar to these birds. Some of the hawk owls have rather long, strong tails reminiscent of hawks, which enable them to turn sharply while flying and catch small birds in flight. But most owls have rather short wings and tails, and for predatory birds are not particularly manoeuvrable or fast. This is no disadvantage, however, because they have a most important adaptation for night hunting – silent flight. Their plumage, including all their flight feathers, is soft and pliable; soft feathers drawn quickly through the air produce no sound.

Sparrow Hawk with
House Sparrow

Feet

In most birds, the feet are simply for walking or hopping or
for supporting the bird's weight while it is at rest. But in
most of the birds of prey and in all the owls, feet have evolved
another important purpose; they are very effective killing
weapons. Some birds of prey also use their beaks to help in
killing their prey, but in nearly all cases the feet are the main
weapons and are often, therefore, highly developed.

The birds of prey have three toes pointing forwards and
one toe pointing backwards (except in the case of one or two
fish eaters). The hind toe and the inside toe are generally
stronger than the others and possess thicker and longer claws.
Most birds of prey can exert an extremely powerful thumb
and forefinger grip with these two toes. The claws are driven
straight into a vulnerable spot on the prey or used to crush it.
Or combined with powerful movements of the legs, they are
used to dislocate the prey's neck; most of the larger hawks,
buzzards and eagles kill by this method. The middle and outer
toes are generally used only to balance the foot while the bird
is perching or walking.

Some of the hawks and falcons which specialize in catching
birds,   however,   have   evolved   a   very   long   middle

toe. This helps the bird to bind to its prey by giving its foot a much wider grip. If the prey turns sharply in flight just as the hawk strikes (which is normally what it will try to do), the hawk's inside claws alone may not be able to grip effectively and the victim might escape.

Some of the birds of prey which kill poisonous snakes have shorter toes than normal to give a very strong, firm grip from which the prey cannot wriggle away. With one or two exceptions, vultures do not have very strong inside toes. When tearing at a carcase, they put their weight on the inside claw which is generally larger than the others. In the American vultures, the hind claw has become very small and is of little use. Most vultures have a

Kite

Harrier eagle

Griffon

Harpy Eagle

Osprey

11

foot somewhat resembling a chicken's to enable them to run quickly on the ground when at a carcase, or when taking off after a heavy meal on a day with no wind. Most kites, which generally feed on small prey or in some cases scavenge like small vultures, have feet which are hardly more specialized than those of vultures.

The Osprey and the Grey-headed and Lesser Fishing Eagles possess two claws facing forwards and two facing backwards. All these birds live mainly by catching fish and use both feet together so that the fish is held with four claws on each side. They also have spine-like scales below their toes, a further adaptation for holding a slippery, wet, wriggling prey.

The adaptation in which the outer toe will reverse to make two toes facing forwards and two facing backwards is also found in all the owls. Owls' feet are not quite as strong as the feet of some of the more rapacious birds of prey, but the claws are often even sharper. Owls use all four claws as offensive weapons to a greater extent than do most of the birds of prey and rarely, if ever, dismember their victims.

Snowy Owl and Norwegian Lemming

12

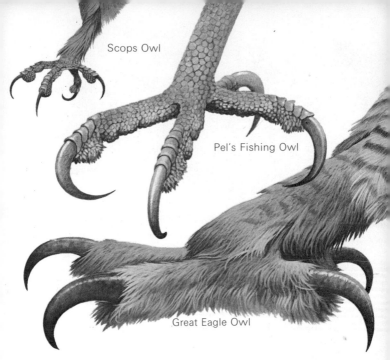

Scops Owl

Pel's Fishing Owl

Great Eagle Owl

Most owls have feathered feet. None of the other birds of prey have the feet covered (although the feathers may nearly cover the toes in the Siberian Golden Eagle) and many have the lower part of the leg completely bare of feathers. However, the two groups of owls which eat fish also have the feet and lower legs bare. The legs often get wet when the birds are hunting and fish scales are difficult to remove from feathers, so this adaptation fits in well with the owls' way of life. These owls also have spine-like scales below the toes, similar to those of the fish-eating birds of prey, which help them to get a firm grip on their prey.

Owls generally prefer to swallow their prey whole and therefore their feet tend to keep clean. As a result, their feathered feet are not a disadvantage to them. In contrast, the feet of the birds of prey are often bloodstained and messy after feeding, as they usually dismember their victims. Bare feet are therefore a great advantage to these birds because they can be cleaned easily and quickly.

Sociable Vulture

Egyptian Vulture

Beaks

The main function of the beak of a bird of prey is to rip its food into pieces which it can swallow. The beak cannot be used to peck, as it can in most birds, because it is the wrong shape. A Golden Eagle has a typical strong, tearing beak. The bird bites so that the hook of the bill is forced into the flesh and then, with both inner claws planted firmly on the prey, the eagle strains back, tearing off a piece of flesh as it does so. The piece is then swallowed and the process repeated.

The beaks of snake eagles are generally smaller because they tend to swallow snakes whole where possible and so do not need to do much tearing. But they have very strong jaw muscles and can bite far harder than can other eagles. This enables them to bite straight through the head of a snake once they have secured a grip near the head with their talons.

Vultures have more variety in the sizes and shapes of their beaks than do any other group. The huge bill of the Sociable Vulture is suitable for tearing off and gulping down huge pieces of muscle. At the other extreme, the small Egyptian Vulture usually arrives last at the carcase and its long slender bill is ideal for extracting small pieces of flesh from between bones which would be overlooked by the larger vultures.

The falcons often use their bills to assist in killing. A falcon has a tooth-like incision in its upper mandible which fits into a notch in the lower mandible and is used to sever the bones at the back of the neck of the victim. Some of the smaller kites have two tooth-like incisions in the upper mandible, which

Golden Eagle

Great
Eagle Owl

are probably an adaptation for dismembering large insects which are held in the foot.

One of the strangest beaks is possessed by the Bat Hawk of Asia and Africa. This hawk hunts at dusk and catches bats and insects in the air with its talons, transfers the catch to its mouth and while still on the wing swallows it whole. The bill has a ridge along the top of the upper mandible and an enormous gape like that of the nightjars.

Owls have rather small, neat beaks, of rather similar shapes. As they swallow much of their prey whole, none has developed a very large beak for tearing flesh. As a result, large owls with big prey tend to take much longer to feed than do eagles for instance. An interesting habit of owls is that they are able to signal aggression by clacking their bills loudly. The lower mandible is extended over the hook of the upper, and then pressed and withdrawn to clap against the upper mandible.

Peregrine Falcon

Cuckoo Falcon

HUNTING AND FEEDING

Hunting Methods

Hunting is a very specialized activity. Birds of prey do not merely fly after something hoping to catch it. If they did, they would achieve nothing except exhaustion. Hunting is difficult and is an art – a large percentage of young birds of prey never become proficient hunters and die during their first few months of independence.

When hunting, a bird of prey tries to find prey which it can catch without using its maximum effort. It therefore looks for something smaller than itself. If it preys on fast-moving birds or large mammals, it seeks something which looks unfit or has become separated from its fellows. Birds of prey are not capable of hunting at maximum effort every day, just as no man can work at peak level all the time. But when times are hard and the birds or their young are very hungry,

Mountain Hawk Eagle above
Musk Deer

Kestrel hovering

they are capable of killing prey in excess of their own size and strength. They prefer not to do this as, apart from the tremendous effort involved, they also risk injuring themselves.

Vultures hunt for dead animals. They fly at great heights from which they often cannot see whether an animal is dead or not. So they watch other carrion-eaters over a wide area, including crows, kites, jackals, hyenas and large carnivores. If a vulture's interest is aroused by something going on below, it will circle lower. This movement will be seen by vultures a mile or so away on each side. If food is definitely available, it will begin to lose height quickly. The birds patrolling within sight will recognize the significance of this and will set their wings into a long fast glide towards the spot the first bird is making for. Vultures further away seeing their neighbours descending will do likewise. Within minutes, many vultures will be arriving at the carcase from all directions at perhaps more than 100 miles an hour.

A common method of hunting is a sort of ambush called 'still' hunting. A bird of prey selects a concealed vantage point, usually in a tree from where it has a good view of the ground below. Any mammal or ground-feeding bird which turns its back to the predator will become vulnerable. This method sounds easy, but skilled timing is essential. A bird diving too fast or too steeply at its prey will need to brake hard before hitting the quarry. This action may create enough noise to cause the quarry to bolt – usually not in the direction the predator is going. To brake and turn together is impossible, and the attack will be unsuccessful.

Small rodents, snakes, and lizards living in flat, open grassland cannot be hunted from a perch unless there are scattered trees. To catch such prey, some birds have evolved the ability to hover. They fly slowly into the wind with wings

beating forwards and the tail depressed and fanned. From their stationary overhead position, the birds detect any small movement in the grass. They usually drop to about fifty feet and hover again before finally plunging feet first onto the prey. The best known European bird of prey, the Kestrel, is an excellent example of this method of hunting.

Another method of hunting over flat country is used by long-winged, lightweight birds of prey, especially where the country undulates slightly or has reed beds or low vegetation. They glide very low over the ground. Every few seconds they make a few flaps to maintain height. Any prey feeding on the ground with its back to the predator may be surprised or be too slow in flying or running for cover to avoid capture. Harriers are typical birds of prey using this method of hunting. They quarter the ground very carefully and patiently, gliding low on wings held in a shallow "V", and pounce on unsuspecting prey. The Marsh Harrier, which hunts over reed-beds, often seems to fall clumsily into the reeds when capturing prey. Some long-winged owls like the Short-eared Owl may often be seen hunting over open marshland in a similar manner for mice and other small rodents.

Gyr Falcon stooping at Ptarmigan

A fast dash, flying very low, is employed by many birds of prey. Those hunting in wooded country have short wings and long tails to enable them to turn rapidly. They will only sight their prey when close to, and the quarry will probably sight them at the same moment and attempt to hurl itself into the nearest cover. The European Sparrow Hawk is a typical short-winged hawk, hunting small birds through woods but frequently alongside hedgerows in wooded country. It flies swiftly along a hedge, first on one side then on the other, and pounces on an unsuspecting victim. But short wings, although letting a bird accelerate very quickly, give no stamina and birds hunting by this method over open country have long wings to enable them to fly fast over long distances.

High soaring flight may be used by some birds to locate prey. The quarry is then watched until it moves into a vulnerable position away from cover. It may of course never do so, and the hunter will have wasted its time. But should it do so, the bird of prey sets off in a rapid glide towards it. After a rapid descent, the bird will have to brake hard with wings and tail before striking and the quarry will get a chance to escape. But if the attacker has timed his move

Verreaux's Eagle and Hyrax

Little Owl and Wood Mouse

correctly the prey will be far from cover and will seldom reach it. Some eagles that live in open country, including the Golden Eagle and the African Martial Eagle, often use this method of hunting. From a high soaring position certain birds of prey are able to catch other birds flying across open country. Following a fast dive, tremendous speed is reached and this often enables the hunter to overtake the quarry before it can reach cover. Many birds of prey use more than one hunting method to obtain their living, and some birds have evolved very specialized methods of their own.

With one or two exceptions, owls are either still hunters or low-level gliders hunting in open country. As is well known, owls have remarkably good eyesight at night. But they have an even more remarkable aid for nocturnal hunting: three-dimensional hearing. Owls possess facial discs shaped to trap sounds, and asymmetrical ears which are located in different positions on each side of the head. Even when hunting on dark moonless nights, most owls are able to locate and strike their quarry by sound alone. But if the prey suddenly becomes stationary or silent, then the eyes of course become necessary. When hunting, owls have the advantage that their prey often cannot see them and still hunters can move their position, their silent flight and the darkness making them undetectable from below.

Another hunting aid possessed by owls is the ability to turn their heads right round in each direction. As a result, they can locate sounds coming from any direction without continually changing their position.

The owls, therefore, generally locate their prey by the senses of sight and, above all, hearing and, taking full advantage of the darkness, fall onto the victim. Their completely noiseless flight gives them the advantage also of being able to take by surprise the unsuspecting animal.

European Eagle Owl with Hedgehog

White-headed Falconet (*left*) and Indian Black Vulture with distended crops

Food

The food requirements of a bird of prey vary according to its size. A tiny pygmy falcon requires about one ounce of food a day, and a large condor will require about one pound.

Smaller birds require far more food compared to their size than do larger birds. The pygmy falcon eats the equivalent of about half its body weight in the course of a day. Because it is very small, its body loses heat rapidly. It is also more active than larger birds of prey. In contrast, the great condor requires only three to four per cent of its body weight of food daily. In the wild this bird probably feeds twice a week on average, although it might return two or three days running to a large carcase and then fast for several days.

A large bird of prey which has been feeding well is able to go two or three weeks without food. A Steller's Sea Eagle at London Zoo which had become overweight voluntarily fasted for six weeks during cold weather. It certainly did it no harm as it has lived there for more than thirty years. Small birds of prey can fast for a day or two, and medium-sized birds become hungry in less than a week even when usually quite fat.

The following table shows the average body weights and food requirements of some birds of prey and owls.

	Weight of Bird		Weekly Food Consumption	
Red-thighed Falconet		1¾ oz		6 oz
Spix Scops Owl		4 oz		7½ oz
American Kestrel		4 oz		8½ oz
European Kestrel		8 oz		10 oz
Tawny Owl	1 lb			12 oz
Peregrine Falcon	1 lb	11 oz	1 lb	4 oz
European Buzzard	2 lb	2 oz	1 lb	4 oz
Short-toed Eagle	4 lb	6 oz	1 lb	13 oz
Great Eagle Owl	6 lb		2 lb	2 oz
Golden Eagle	8 lb	4 oz	3 lb	3 oz
Lammergeyer	12 lb	8 oz	4 lb	
Andean Condor	25 lb		6 lb	12 oz

The table gives a rough guide to the requirements of various sizes of birds of prey and owls. Of course, there is quite a difference among individuals, just as there is among people.

Most birds will need to kill prey weighing appreciably more than the food weight indicated in the table, unless they swallow their prey whole. The amount of a carcase left uneaten varies according to the species of predator, how hungry it is, and what the prey happens to be. Sometimes, of course, other predators or scavengers may feed from the carcase if it is a large one, forcing the bird of prey to kill again before it would otherwise have been necessary.

Young birds of prey eat nothing on the day that they hatch. The head is rather unsteady and, as they have to reach up and take the morsel offered by the mother bird (they do not gape like many young birds do), they are probably unable to feed then. By the second day the neck muscles are stronger, and they are able to take food offered to them. The appetite increases very quickly in many of the smaller birds, and more slowly in some of the larger species which will take longer to reach maturity.

A young Black-shouldered Kite aged sixteen days can weigh more than its parent – it is by no means fully developed, but is very fat. At the other extreme, the young of large vultures may not reach their adult weight by four months. Tropical birds of prey grow more slowly than do their temperate relatives because their parents have a shorter day to do their hunting in. By the time birds of prey are half grown, they may be eating more than twice the amount of food required by their parents. They do little but eat and sleep at this time unless disturbed by other members of their brood.

Birds that spend most of their flying time soaring or still hunting tend to eat slightly less than do birds which use more energy beating their wings rapidly when chasing their quarry, as would be expected. But not all birds require more food on entering a period of increased activity. Some merely lose a little weight as their muscles harden, and their appetites remain the same.

Birds of prey living in cold countries are usually larger and have many more downy feathers than do related species from warm countries. Their appetites generally increase by about a tenth in very cold weather.

Golden Eagle — newly hatched, half grown and nearly fledged

Pellets

As we have already seen, owls prefer to swallow their prey whole, and many birds of prey will also do so, especially if the prey is small. Even with large prey, from which most of the fur or feathers may be plucked, a considerable amount of indigestible material accumulates in the bird's gizzard and forms a firm pellet. The pellet is bound together with the swallowed fur or feathers to form a cylindrical capsule that can be passed up the bird's digestive tract. This regurgitation is accomplished with the aid of a reaching movement by the bird, with the head being pumped up and down.

Pellets are normally ejected by a bird eight to twenty-four hours after a meal, but sometimes are retained for up to five days. Insects and other invertebrates' remains are also found in pellets, and some small hawks and owls have pellets consisting mainly of these.

It is not uncommon to find that a pellet recently disgorged appears shiny. This is caused by a mucous secretion which doubtless must help the bird to eject the pellet.

Owls seem generally unable to digest bones, and if one of their pellets is examined the whole skeleton of the prey may be found inside. This makes it easy for scientists to discover what owls eat. If they find where an owl is roosting, it is a simple matter to collect the pellets and examine them.

Most birds of prey can digest small bones, and some break down surprisingly large ones. If a small animal or bird has been eaten, there may be no trace of bones at all in the pellet. In

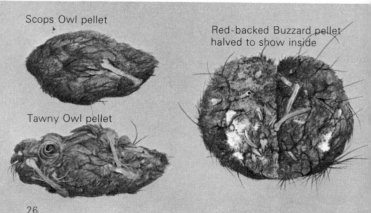

Scops Owl pellet

Tawny Owl pellet

Red-backed Buzzard pellet halved to show inside

other birds, when large bones have been eaten and softened, partly digested bone may be ejected – not always in the form of a pellet, as certain birds of prey throw up softened bones in tiny fragments. Pellets also assist in keeping the bird's digestive tract healthy. The soft fur or feathers on the outside of the pellet act rather like a swab, cleaning the walls as it passes on the way to be shaken or dropped out.

Material for pellet formation seems definitely important to the health of most birds, especially while they are young. As birds grow older however, pellets sometimes become unnecessary and they avoid eating indigestible parts of their prey. Occasionally fur or feathers may even be harmful.

The best place to find pellets is in the vicinity of the nesting or roosting area – in fact, the presence of pellets is often the first clue that a particular bird is nesting, or roosting nearby. There are, obviously, certain variations between the pellets of an individual bird, depending on what food was eaten on the previous day or night, but birds often regurgitate pellets that are sufficiently characteristic to enable them to be identified.

Examination of the contents of pellets will reveal what the bird in question has been eating recently, but to gain some proper idea of the bird's diet, a careful examination throughout the year is necessary.

Owls and birds of prey are not the only birds to eject pellets. Herons, kingfishers, curlews and a variety of other birds which cannot fully digest the whole of their diet (which may often consist of fish, for example) expel the indigestible parts.

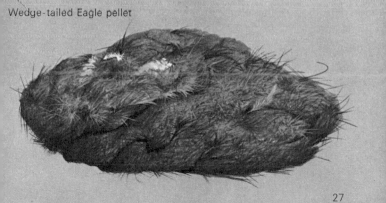

Wedge-tailed Eagle pellet

SEXUAL DIMORPHISM

In some birds of prey, the hen and cock birds are of approximately the same size. But in most, and in the owls, the females are larger than the males, some hens weighing almost twice as much as their mates. This difference, known as sexual dimorphism, may seem rather strange, but there are very good reasons why it should exist, which research has proved to us.

In some species, such as those that feed entirely or mainly off carrion or on snakes, the food taken by both sexes is identical. The methods of locating the food, and of hunting and killing it are also the same whichever sex the bird happens to be. In the case of species which hunt birds or mammals, however, the situation is often quite different.

Brown Harrier Eagles

male

female

Sparrow Hawks

The majority of birds of prey and nearly all owls have territories which are usually rather ill-defined, but in practice the hunting range of the pair of birds is limited. This, in turn, will limit the number of birds or animals that it is possible to hunt. The Northern Sparrow Hawk is a good example. The male is a tiny bird compared to his mate, but is extremely active and very fast and manoeuvrable over short distances. He specializes in catching small birds up to the size of a thrush. The female on the other hand is appreciably larger, much heavier and stronger. She tends to be less active and a little slower, but is more of a specialist in catching medium-sized birds from thrushes to partridges or even a pigeon if it happens to be rather slow or weak. As a result, a pair of birds of dissimilar size are able to live off a territory which would not support two identical birds when times are hard.

When food is scarce, perhaps in the shorter days of winter when the weather is bad, or in times of prolonged drought in the tropics, the female may kill prey larger than normal. She may share it with the male. On the other hand, the male may be able to catch something fast-moving, perhaps right at the limit of his capabilities, which he will share with the female.

We have found a reason why one sex should be larger than the other, but this does not explain why the larger bird should be the female. There are also good reasons why this should be

29

Peregrine Falcons — female (*front*) snatching pigeon from male

so. All birds of prey and owls have a natural tendency to want to keep their food to themselves; this is of course very necessary. As young birds in the nest, they learn to keep their food away from their nest mates. And as adults, they learn to defend their catch from other predators which may attempt to rob them. When bringing prey to the nest, male birds are sometimes rather reluctant to release the food, especially if they are a little hungry themselves. The female, being the larger, is generally dominant over the male and is able to take prey from him if necessary.

When the young are first hatched, they are brooded for most of the time by the female who will generally remain on guard at the nest all the time. The value of having the larger and more aggressive parent left to guard the young while they are small is obvious. During this time, the young require only a moderate amount of food; but it must be of very good quality, generally heart, liver and muscle from prey at the smaller end of the range. For example, several small birds such as tits and finches are better food for young Sparrow Hawks than perhaps a pigeon, although the latter would certainly contain as much nourishment.

The male Sparrow Hawk is more agile and active than his mate, and he can catch more small prey in the course of a day than she can. As soon as the young begin to develop quickly, the female ceases to brood them (except at night or in bad weather) and begins hunting herself. At this stage the young need appreciably more food than do the adults, and the female's capacity to catch larger prey becomes very important. The young then eat every part of the carcase of almost any food that is provided, to enable them to keep up a maximum rate of growth.

Many of these birds are by nature aggressive and solitary and the co-operation required to rear a brood may well be extremely difficult. The reversal in sizes is possibly an adaptation to ensure survival of the species, the male at the nest being dominated by the female who has the important task of looking after the young in the early stages.

Goshawks — male bringing thrush to nest

Bataleur female and nest (*opposite*)

NESTING AND TRAINING THE YOUNG

Pre-nesting and Incubation

Nearly all birds of prey and owls seem to take an interest in their nesting sites for some time before the female actually begins to lay eggs. In the case of some of the larger birds of prey, this interest may start several months before laying commences. They may start spending time near the nest and, if it is a large structure, add branches and begin to re-arrange it. Many birds of prey have alternative nest sites, generally two or three or occasionally even more. This arrangement is probably an adaptation to aid sanitation, or to prevent continued infestation by nest parasites, lice, and flies. Many birds of prey use the same nest year after year, whereas some choose a new site every breeding season. In some species or individuals which return to use the same site and the same nest for some years in succession, the nest itself becomes a huge structure as the material is augmented each spring with extra branches and twigs.

Probably the majority of birds of prey and owls pair for life. But should one of the pair die, then the other will often get a new mate fairly quickly, unless it belongs to a species which is rare in the surrounding area. Other pairs which disperse or migrate will normally return each year to the same nest site at breeding time, and so generally will meet and pair with their mate of the previous year.

During courtship most birds of prey put on aerial displays for the benefit of their mates. In the case of most owls, of course, darkness makes this behaviour pointless. So they generally sit together, occasionally rubbing their beaks together and calling. Many birds of prey preen each other during courtship, although this seldom happens among the more aggressive species. Most of the larger birds bring a green leafy branch to their mate at the nest, and this 'present' seems somehow to excite both birds.

When the female is about to lay, she stops feeding and begins brooding. After the egg or eggs are laid she incubates them most of the time. Sometimes the male sits on the eggs, individual pairs varying in this respect. The male normally provides the female with food, although she needs less than usual at this time. She may have to incubate for between 14 and 52 days, depending on the species.

Golden Eagle's nest in pine tree

Nests

Birds of prey and owls may build their nests almost anywhere. Ideally the nest should be in a place that other predators cannot easily reach, sheltered from wind and rain, and from hot sunshine, and it should be a safe cradle for eggs and young.

Probably the best sited of all nests are in holes, or on a sheltered ledge on a crag. A hole may be in a tree, in a building, or even in the ground. Or it may be a small cave on a mountainside. These sites generally possess all the above advantages; the nests also require less material and are easier to build than most other kinds.

Many of the birds of prey which nest in trees prefer to use the vacated nests of other species, as do some owls. But many, including all the eagles, build their own nests and these may be enormous structures. They are added to year after year, until they become so heavy that they fall, usually in a gale or sometimes the tree is unable to withstand the weight of the nest and it topples over. One Golden Eagle's eyrie in a pine tree was seventeen feet deep and five feet across. Nests about ten feet deep may contain more than a ton of sticks.

A tree nest in a sheltered site may last for many years – a nest of a Crowned Hawk Eagle in South Africa has been in use for more than 70 years. A tree nest has the advantage of giving shade to the sitting bird and its young, as long as it is not on the top-most branches, but it is generally less sheltered and safe than most crag nests.

Certain birds of prey and owls build nests in large cactus-like plants with sharp spines and sometimes poisonous sap. These sites minimize danger from the ground but nests on top are exposed to the sun and vulnerable to attack from the air.

Quite a large number of raptorial birds nest on the ground in steppe or desert country. And in marshland, there is often no alternative site. The nest may simply be on a rise in the ground, or in a small pile of stones, a reed bed or other thick cover. On islands where there are few predators, birds of prey may nest on the shore.

Osprey's nest on island shore and (*below*) Cape Vulture's nest on cliff ledge

Eggs

Birds of prey and owls lay fewer eggs than do most other orders of birds. Many of the larger species lay only one or two eggs, and not all birds of prey lay every year. Most of the smaller kinds lay between three and five eggs.

In the Arctic, birds of prey and owls lay up to nine eggs when prey is plentiful, as in a year when lemmings swarm. But when prey is scarce they may lay only one or two or often no eggs at all. Both kinds of raptorial birds lay eggs of a size in proportion to the hen's size. Natural selection would not favour birds producing a large egg because a female bird making a kill while carrying an egg inside her might easily break it, which would probably be fatal to her. Birds of prey in captivity lose their appetites a day or two before they lay, probably for this reason. On the other hand, no bird of prey can lay a small egg, because the young must be sufficiently developed when hatched to be able to eat and digest raw meat.

The eggs of birds of prey are rounded at one end and rather pointed at the other. This shape will not tend to roll out of a stick nest or off a rocky ledge. Many eggs are beautifully marked with reddish browns, sometimes almost orange, and various other shades of brown, sometimes nearly purple. Others are white or almost white, although many of these – including those of most eagles – are pale green when first laid but fade to white after two or three days. There is considerable variation in the markings of eggs in some species.

Owls' eggs are, however, quite different. Although they sometimes nest in the nests of other birds, most owls nest in holes. As a result the eggs are unlikely to roll out, and so they are almost completely round; the evolution of a more complicated shape has been unnecessary. And nesting in holes as they do they require no camouflage to hide them from predators, so they are invariably white.

As might be expected, the largest eggs are those of the Andean and California Condor, measuring $4\frac{1}{4}$ inches by $2\frac{2}{3}$ inches. The eggs of the larger eagles measure about 3 inches by $2\frac{1}{3}$ inches and weigh five to six ounces. Some other sizes, in inches, are: Buzzard $2\frac{1}{4}$x$1\frac{3}{4}$, Kestrel $1\frac{3}{5}$x$1\frac{1}{4}$, Red-thighed Falconet $1\frac{1}{6}$x$\frac{7}{8}$, Great Eagle Owl $2\frac{1}{3}$x2, Barn Owl $1\frac{3}{5}$x$1\frac{1}{4}$, and Pygmy Owl $1\frac{1}{6}$x1.

White-tailed
Sea Eagle

Egyptian Vulture

Tawny Owl

Kestrel

Great Eagle Owl

Bat Falcon dropping Black-
throated Green Warbler
to young

38

Care and Training of Young

Good parents are perhaps even more important to young birds of prey than they are to any other creatures, including human beings. We have already seen how the young are cared for continually by the mother, while the father provides all the food, until the stage is reached when the family needs so much food that the female must herself begin hunting again. As the young get larger, they begin to learn to dismember carcases for themselves. Prey is merely brought into the nest and left there by the adults. This is the first real work the young learn to do; it is the first stage towards independence.

Young birds of prey are not normally starved into leaving the nest. They often practise flapping their wings at the edge of the nest, and sometimes leave accidently in a gust of wind. Sometimes the sight of a parent or brother or sister feeding on a nearby branch will provide the incentive, but usually they seem suddenly to make up their minds to go and they are off.

The first flight is uncertain and landings are generally awkward for some time, but flying ability steadily improves with continual practice. With species that live entirely off flying prey, a very high flying standard must be reached and the parents continue to help for some time. With species that feed off carrion or slow-moving prey, complete independence may be achieved rather earlier.

Often adult birds play aerial games with their young, one bird chasing the next – diving, twisting, looping, making sharp turns and other manoeuvres at speed. Sometimes the parent carries prey and encourages the young to go for it. The parent of course eventually releases the prey, but not before the young one has had to struggle, for it must learn that prey does not give itself up easily. Parent birds often attempt to improve the young's skill by passing food to it in mid-air, or by dropping food for it to catch. Young birds will attempt to catch any falling objects, such as leaves, feathers and flying insects, and so increase their skill.

At first they will be able to catch food for themselves only occasionally, and their parents still feed them. But gradually their ability increases and they become more independent. This process may take only a few weeks, or in the case of some of the eagles it takes as much as a year.

SYSTEMATIC LIST OF BIRDS OF PREY AND OWLS

American Vultures

The seven surviving species of the family Cathartidae, the American — Cathartid — Vultures, are the descendants of a once much more widespread group of birds. They were probably once found throughout the world and fossil remains have been found in Europe. Numerous fossil remains have also been found in California, including some species far larger than any vultures living today. One of these, *Teratornis incredibilis*, had a wing span of 17 feet. Others, including *Teratornis merriami*, which only became extinct comparatively recently, possessed a wing spread of 12 to 14 feet.

Birds of this size could survive only in ideal surroundings. They would require a large amount of food as well as good weather conditions in which to glide and soar. Taking off would also be difficult when the bird had a full crop.

Two very large members of the family have survived however. They are the Great or Andean Condor (*Vultur gryphus*) and the California Condor (*Gymnogyps californianus*), both 40 to 46 inches in length. Both birds are similar also in wing spread, spanning 9 to 10 feet and weighing from 20 to 28 pounds. The Andean Condor is found throughout almost all the Andes Mountains from sea level to over 15,000 feet. Although it has declined in some areas, it still holds its own in many places. It feeds mostly on carrion – dead llamas, cattle, sheep, and so on, and where it comes down to the shore in remote areas it will feed on such things as stranded marine mammals, including whales. It is an extremely strong bird,

King Vulture

Andean Condor

Red-headed Turkey Vulture

Greater Yellow-headed Turkey Vulture

and has been known to kill sick llamas and even horses if it is really hungry. Young birds are brown, adults are black and silver-grey. This is the only species of American vulture which may be sexed easily as the male has a yellow eye and a wattle above the beak. The female lacks this and has a red eye.

Probably the nearest relative of the Andean Condor is the King Vulture (*Sarcohamphus papa*). Measuring 30 to 32 inches long, it is a smaller bird with a wing spread of about 6 feet or a little more. It is an inhabitant of tropical forests from Mexico to northern Argentina. It does not ascend the mountains as it cannot withstand frost, but in other respects is a strong bird, driving other vultures from carrion and apparently able to kill snakes. Young birds are brown and adults at six years are black and pinkish-white, with an orange wattle on a dark head.

The American Black Vulture (*Coragyps atratus*) is a small vulture, 22 to 26 inches long, with a wing spread of only a little more than 4 feet and weighing $4\frac{1}{2}$ pounds. These birds are gregarious and tend to congregate where food is likely to be abundant. Being a short-winged bird, it spends less time in the air than do other species and so is not able to search a very large area. Although normally entirely a carrion eater feeding on dead animals, fish washed up on the shore, and garbage on

dumps, it will occasionally eat birds' eggs and has been known to kill young pigs.

There are three species of turkey vulture, the Red-headed Turkey Vulture (*Cathartes aura*), 26 to 30 inches, which ranges from southern Canada to Tierra del Fuego and the Falkland Islands, and two tropical South American species, the Yellow-headed Turkey Vulture (*Cathartes burrovianus*), 22 to 26 inches, and the Greater Yellow-headed Turkey Vulture (*Cathartes melambrotus*), 28 to 32 inches.

Turkey vultures are long-winged birds with a 6-foot span, except for the Yellow-headed which has short wings. They soar high and fly low over the ground, like harriers, searching for carrion. They can find carrion (providing it is not fresh) by scent when flying low, and are the only vultures able to do this.

The California Condor is really a gigantic turkey vulture, now sadly reduced to about forty birds living in remote parts of California. They breed in caves high up on mountains in similar sites to those of the Andean Condor. The smaller American vultures generally breed near or on the ground among bushes, rocks, and in hollow trees or occasionally in old ruins. The condors lay only one egg and do not breed every year. The smaller vultures generally breed annually.

Secretary Bird and Osprey

The Secretary Bird (*Sagittarius serpentarius*) lives in savannah country south of the Sahara in Africa. It is really a kind of pedestrian bird of prey. Perched on its long stilt-like legs, it is able to examine the ground it is hunting far more thoroughly than any other bird of prey. It is probably best known because of its ability to catch snakes, but it searches the grassland for a very wide variety of food which includes large numbers of insects, as well as small rodents, young birds, lizards, and so on. Because the feet are less specialized than those of many other birds of prey – owing to the fact that they are its main means of locomotion when hunting – it has evolved a different method of killing its prey. This it does by a very hard stamp; it usually leaps back a yard or so after each stamp and circles the prey, then jumps in again giving another blow with one foot. The method is very safe against snakes. The claws may be used to assist in killing prey, but to a lesser extent than in most other birds of prey. Secretary Birds fly less than most other raptorial birds, and generally keep low, seldom soaring. Two eggs are laid in a rather small nest, usually on a low, flat-topped bush.

Secretary Bird with python

The Osprey (*Pandion haliaetus*), 23 to 24 inches in length, is the most specialized of the birds of prey at catching fish. Its well-adapted foot, with two toes facing in each direction, and sharply pointed scales below each claw enable it to grip the slippery, wriggling fish. It will sometimes still hunt from a perch beside a lake, but usually flies fairly low in a rather kite-like manner, and immediately hovers upon sighting a movement in the water below. Should the movement be made by a fish of the right size swimming near the surface, the Osprey dives. It enters the water feet first and can submerge if necessary to clutch its quarry. It is the only bird of prey able to do so and its plumage is extremely waterproof. Large fish have been caught with the skeleton of an Osprey attached to their backs, showing that the birds occasionally strike quarry which is too strong for them. Ospreys are found almost throughout the world, except in the polar regions. They breed usually on islands, sometimes in very dense colonies. Their two or three eggs are laid in a large nest made of branches, seaweed, driftwood or dead vegetable matter on a tree, old building, or on the ground in certain types of country.

Osprey

Black Baza

Kites

Cuckoo falcons or bazas are small birds, 15 to 17 inches long, which inhabit forest areas in Africa and Madagascar, parts of south-eastern Asia, and northern Australasia. They hunt most often at dawn and dusk, and sometimes move in small parties, searching the trees for small prey. They take bats occasionally. Their most unusual feature is the possession of two serrations in the upper mandible, an adaptation which assists them in holding and dismembering large insects, and probably helps when killing larger prey as their feet are rather weak.

There are five species and all have crests. The African Cuckoo Falcon (*Aviceda cuculoides*) is brown above with a greyish head and chest, and white below banded with rufous. The Madagascar Cuckoo Falcon (*Aviceda madagascariensis*) has three black stripes on the throat and is white below with rufous streaks. Jerdon's Baza (*Aviceda jerdoni*), found from Sikkim to Sumatra, has a black crest tipped with white. And the Crested Baza (*Aviceda subcristata*) of Australia and nearby islands has a shorter crest, with rufous thighs and underwings. The Black Baza (*Aviceda leuphotes*) inhabits much of India, Burma and Malaya and is much smaller than the others (11 inches).

Two small hawks inhabiting South American jungle, the Double-toothed Kite (*Harpagus bidentatus*), 12 to 14 inches, and the Rufous-thighed Kite (*H. diodon*), 12 to 14 inches, are similar in habits to the cuckoo falcons. They too have double-toothed beaks. The sexes are quite different in the Double-toothed Kite; males are dark brown above, greyer on the head, and barred-grey and white below. Females are brown below with white barring on the belly. The Rufous-thighed Kite, apart from its thighs, is light grey below.

The Bat-eating Buzzard (*Machaerhamphus alcinus*), 16 to 19 inches, of southern Africa, Indonesia and New Guinea, is the most nocturnal of all birds of prey. It resembles a large, dark cuckoo falcon and has very long wings, giving it the great speed it requires to catch its quarry. As well as killing bats, it takes insects and the occasional small bird. It spends the day resting on the branch of a tree. Like the

Bat-eating Buzzard diving at bat

other species in this category, it builds a nest in a tree, generally producing two eggs. Cuckoo falcons lay from one to three eggs and Double-toothed Kites from three to four.

Another kite with a pronounced tooth on its upper mandible is the Cayenne or Grey-headed Kite (*Leptodon cayanensis*), 17 to 20 inches, which lives in lowland forests from southern Mexico to northern Argentina. It has large wings and a long, black and pale grey barred tail. It is black above, white below, and has a light grey head. Little seems to be known about it. It is reputed to catch small birds but is probably insectivorous.

The Hook-billed Kite (*Chondrohierax uncinatus*), 14 to 15 inches, inhabits the same area. Males are dark slate above, and grey, narrowly barred with white or sandy, or completely grey below. Females have slaty heads and a reddish half collar, and are sandy, barred brown below. Sometimes both sexes are bluish-slate all over. It feeds on large tree snails, insects, reptiles and birds.

The Snail Kite (*Rostrhamus sociabilis*), 15½ to 16½ inches, is found over a similar area to the two previous kites but also in Florida and Cuba. It feeds entirely on freshwater snails, its long hooked bill being specially adapted to extract these from their shells. The male is shown in the illustration; females are deep brown, the underparts streaked lighter, and have a white streak over each eye and a white rump.

The Slender-billed Kite (*R. hamatus*) of northern South America is slightly smaller, with an even longer bill and

Honey Buzzard

stronger legs and feet. It has dark plumage throughout. Its habits are the same as those of the Snail Kite. Snail Kites nest in scattered colonies, usually in rushes. Two to four eggs are laid.

The Honey Buzzard (*Pernis apivorus*), 20 to 24 inches, is really a kite which superficially resembles a buzzard. It is found in summer almost throughout Europe and Asia from Britain to Borneo. In winter it moves into Africa and southern Asia where many of the resident birds may be distinguished by the possession of a crest. The plumage of this species is however very variable throughout its range. The Barred Honey Buzzard (*P. celebensis*), 20 to 22 inches, of Celebes and the Philippines is heavily barred brown and white below. These birds raid the nests of wasps and bees for grubs and honeycomb but will also take mammals and birds. They usually use old nests of other birds but sometimes they build their own. Two eggs are usual.

The Long-tailed Honey Buzzard (*Henicopernis longicauda*), 20 to 22 inches, of New Guinea and surrounding islands, is dark brown above barred with grey, and whitish with dark streaks below. Little is known about it, and it probably lays only one egg. Birds on New Britain are smaller (18 inches long) and darker and are perhaps a distinct species, known as the Black or Gurney's Honey Buzzard (*H. infuscata*).

The Plumbeous Kite (*Ictinia plumbea*), 15 inches, inhabits open country with groups of tall trees from Mexico to northern Argentina. It is dark grey above and pale grey below

Snail Kite

with two white bars on the tail. The Mississippi Kite (*I. misisippiensis*), 14 inches, found in the south-eastern United States in summer, migrating south in winter, is similar but with the tail entirely black. These kites look like falcons in flight, hawking for insects high in the air. They generally nest in high trees, laying one to three eggs in number.

The Swallow-tailed Kite (*Elanoides forficatus*), 24 inches, is found on low ground near water from the southern United States to northern Argentina. This beautiful bird is often seen in small flocks soaring high in the air, where it captures large insects. It will also take tree frogs, lizards, and occasionally snakes from the upper branches of trees. It nests high in tall trees, laying two or three eggs.

The African Swallow-tailed Kite (*Chelictinia riocourii*), 15 inches, is found from Senegal across Africa to the Sudan and Kenya in open country. It looks very graceful and slender in flight. The plumage is light grey above and white below. It lives mainly on insects, and is usually seen in small flocks

Swallow-tailed Kite

hawking them high in the air, but will take them from the ground along with occasional lizards and mice. It makes a nest in a small thorn tree where it lays its three or four eggs.

The Pearl Kite (*Gampsonyx swainsonii*), 8 inches, lives in lightly wooded savannah and open forest edges in northern and central South America. Its plumage is dark brown and grey mixed above, rufous on neck and side, and white with black patches below. Its food consists of insects, lizards and occasionally mice and small birds. It breeds in tall trees in small colonies, each nest containing three eggs.

The Black-shouldered Kite (*Elanus caeruleus*), 11 to 14 inches, is found in Portugal, Africa and south-eastern Asia. The White-tailed Kite (*E. leucurus*), 16 inches, of the New World and the Australian Black-shouldered Kite (*E. notatus*), 13 to 14 inches, are very similar. The two last show a black mark under the wing joint, otherwise the colours vary only slightly. The Letter-winged Kite (*E. scriptus*) of south and central Australia is similar to the Black-shouldered but has a black bar running along the forward edge of the wing. Rats and other small rodents are the main food, also small reptiles and frogs and occasionally birds. It generally flies slowly when hunting, hovering frequently. It also still hunts from trees, wires, and poles. These last four kites all build small nests in trees, generally laying three to four eggs.

The size of the Black Kite (*Milvus migrans*) varies between

Black-shouldered Kite hovering

Black Kite

18 and 25 inches in different areas and it is one of the two commonest birds of prey, being found over most of the Old World from Spain to Australia. It is light in weight – between 1 and $1\frac{1}{2}$ pounds – and its long wings and tail give it a wonderful buoyant flight. It soars for much of the day and descends to pick up any small piece of food, whether alive or dead. It usually nests in trees, or occasionally on rocks or buildings, sometimes several pairs together. Three eggs form the usual clutch. The Red Kite (*M. milvus*), 22 to 24 inches, is found in central Wales, most of Europe, north-eastern Africa and the

Red Kite – flight silhouette

Cape Verde Islands. It is a more majestic bird than the Black Kite, with even longer wings and tail, and is reddish-brown in colour. It takes a variety of food but kills bigger prey than the Black Kite. It builds its nest in trees, and three eggs are usual.

The Square-tailed Kite (*Lophoictinia isura*), of Australia, which is 20 inches in size, is rather similar to the Red Kite but the tail is shorter and only slightly notched. It flies lower than do most kites when hunting – rather like a harrier – and catches young birds, reptiles, and even caterpillars. It lays two or three eggs in tree nests, which it usually builds near water.

The Black-breasted Kite (*Hamirostra melanosternon*), 21 to 24 inches, is another Australian species, heavier built than the last species and with a short tail. Some birds are similar in colouring to the Square-tailed Kite; others have black heads and breasts. It preys mainly on rabbits and lizards. It also eats eggs and will break an Emu's egg with a stone. It nests in trees where it lays two eggs.

The Brahminy Kite (*Haliastur indus*), 17 to 20 inches, is found from India to northern Australia, and the Whistling Kite or Whistling Eagle (*H. sphenurus*), 20 to 22 inches, is found over most of Australia, New Guinea and some other islands. The latter is a brown bird with buffish markings. Both birds will eat almost any sorts of animals from locusts and other insects to fish (dead or alive), frogs, reptiles, young birds and small mammals. Some Whistling Kites regularly catch rabbits. Both species live near water, on the coast or inland. They nest in a tree, laying two or sometimes three eggs.

Brahminy Kite

Sea Eagles

The eight species of sea eagles are quite closely related to kites but are far more massive and much heavier. They have therefore developed much broader wings to keep them airborne. The wing span is large, varying between 5½ and 7½ feet. Their tails are mostly wedge-shaped. There are four smaller sea eagles. The White-bellied Sea Eagle (*Haliaeetus leucogaster*), 25 to 27 inches, which is found on sea coasts from India to Australia is grey above with head and underparts white. Sanford's Sea Eagle (*H. sanfordi*), 25 to 28 inches, of the Solomon Islands, is dark brown above and rufous brown below. The African Sea Eagle (*H. vocifer*), 23 to 29 inches, is found on coasts, lakes and rivers in Africa south of the Sahara. The Madagascar Sea Eagle (*H. vociferoides*), 23 to 26 inches, is mainly brown with rufous streaking on the head and underparts; its cheeks and tail are white.

The four larger sea eagles are: Pallas's Sea Eagle (*H.*

White-tailed Sea Eagle

leucoryphus), 27 to 32 inches, found from the Caspian Sea to the Amur River and in south to central India and Burma. It is brown with a buff head and neck, and a broad white band across the rounded tail. The Bald Eagle (*H. leucocephalus*) of North America is 30 to 36 inches in size and dark brown with a pure white head. The White-tailed or Grey Sea Eagle (*H. albicilla*), 27 to 38 inches, is found in Greenland, Iceland, much of Europe, and in northern and central Asia. It used to breed in Britain. Steller's Sea Eagle (*H. pelagicus*), 35 to 41 inches, comes from north-eastern Asia. Besides the bird illustrated here, there is an all-black colour phase with a white tail.

Sea eagles take a wide range of prey. The smaller species eat

Steller's Sea Eagle

mostly fish, which they take within a foot of the surface. Sanford's Sea Eagle also takes birds and mammals.

The larger sea eagles eat more carrion, and catch large birds and mammals. Most prey taken is sick, injured or immature as sea eagles are not very manoeuvrable. Sea eagles are among the most noisy birds of prey. When giving loud calls they throw their heads right back. Their huge nests are built on trees, cliff ledges, islands, among rocks, or on the ground in remote treeless areas. Normally two eggs are laid, sometimes only one, but Pallas's Sea Eagle generally lays three.

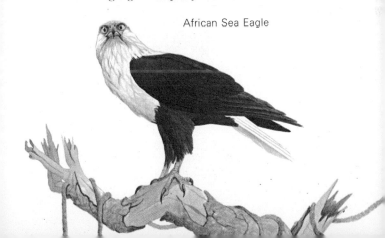

African Sea Eagle

Fishing Eagles

The Grey-headed Fishing Eagle (*Icthyophaga ichthyaetus*), 24 to 29 inches, is found over most of India, Ceylon and Burma down to Celebes, including the Philippines. The Lesser Fishing Eagle (*I. nana*), 20 to 26 inches, inhabits northern India, Burma, the Malay peninsula, Sumatra and Borneo. It is similar in colour to the Grey-headed Fishing Eagle but has the tail completely dark brown. These fishing eagles inhabit lakes, rivers, marshes and in the case of the Grey-headed, the sea coast. They live almost entirely on fish but have been known to take reptiles, ground birds and small mammals. Their outer claw is reversible like the Osprey's and they have similar pointed scales below the toes – adaptations for grasping wriggling fish. Unlike the sea eagles these birds have short wings, 3 feet 9 inches to 5 feet across. It is not surprising therefore

Grey-headed Fishing Eagle

Vulturine Fish Eagle

that they spend most of the day sitting in a tree, seldom flying far. They catch fish within a foot of the surface as do sea eagles, and like those birds they can be noisy. They often call at night. Their nests are in tall trees and they lay sometimes one, usually two, or occasionally three eggs.

The Vulturine Fish Eagle or Palm Nut Vulture (*Gypohierax angolensis*), 22 to 25 inches, can be found over much of Africa south of the Sahara. Its distribution depends on the presence of the oil palm and raffia palm, the nuts of which are important items in its diet. It also eats fish (generally dead ones), crabs and small carrion, but has a strong foot and has been known to kill mammals of about its own weight – that is, 3 to 4 pounds. It has a variety of call notes, coughs, mews, growls and other calls very similar to the last species. It builds a large nest in a tall tree or in the hollowed out centre of the huge nut clusters of the raffia palm. It lays only one egg.

During the nesting season these birds perform aerial dives from very high up, in a manner similar to the sea eagles.

Vultures

The White-headed Vulture (*Trigonoceps occipitalis*), 30 to 32 inches, is found over most of Africa south of Sierra Leone and the Sudan. It is less of a true vulture than any of the following species. They are usually solitary or in pairs, sometimes accompanied by an immature bird. They look more eagle-like than do other vultures. The tail is square, making them more manoeuvrable, and they have a fairly strong foot – adaptations enabling them to kill the young of small antelopes and such birds as young Lesser Flamingos. When hungry, they can drive most other vultures from carcases.

The Cinereous Vulture (*Aegypius monachus*), 42 to 45 inches,

Left:
1 Ruppell's Griffon
2 Immature Ruppell's Griffon
3 Lappet-faced Vulture
4 Immature Lappet-faced Vulture
5 White-headed Vulture
6 Egyptian Vulture
7 White-backed Vulture
8 Hooded Vultures

Griffon Vulture (*right*)

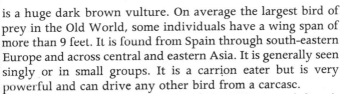

is a huge dark brown vulture. On average the largest bird of prey in the Old World, some individuals have a wing span of more than 9 feet. It is found from Spain through south-eastern Europe and across central and eastern Asia. It is generally seen singly or in small groups. It is a carrion eater but is very powerful and can drive any other bird from a carcase.

The Lappet-faced or Sociable Vulture (*Torgos tracheliotus*), 40 to 45 inches, is another vulture generally seen singly or in family groups. Found over most of the drier parts of Africa and in Palestine, it is dominant over all other African vultures when hungry. Its huge beak enables it to tear off and gulp down large pieces of muscle.

The Pondicherry or Indian Black Vulture (*Sarcogyps calvus*), 30 to 32 inches, is found over most of India, Burma and the Malay peninsula. It is a black vulture with huge reddish lappets of skin hanging from the face and patches of white down on the chest and above the thighs. These birds are usually seen in pairs. Owing to its small size, it is not dominant at carcases, but with its large bill it can tear off sufficient food for itself very rapidly.

The four solitary vultures just described all build large nests high in a tree and normally lay only one egg.

Griffons are large vultures which live in colonies in mountainous country. There are five species: the Himalayan Griffon Vulture (*Gyps himalayensis*), 41 to 43 inches, is on average the second largest bird of prey in the Old World. It is a huge brownish-white bird with a wing span of about 9 feet. The Griffon Vulture (*G. fulvus*), 39 to 41 inches, is a darker bird found from Spain across to northern India. The Cape Griffon Vulture (*G. coprotheres*), 39 to 41 inches, of South

Bearded Vulture *or* Lammergeyer

Africa is similar but paler. Ruppell's Griffon (*G. ruppellii*), 35 to 37 inches, is found from Gambia to Kenya and north to Egypt. It is a brownish-black bird with whitish spots. Lastly the Long-billed Vulture (*G. indicus*) of India, Burma, and Malaysia, 32 to 34 inches in size, is pale below with either a dark or pale brown back. Griffons nest and roost in colonies on cliff ledges, leaving there late in the morning to search for food and returning late in the afternoon – although there are generally some birds flying all day. They occasionally nest in trees and usually lay only one egg.

The African White-backed Vulture (*G. africanus*), 30 inches, and the Indian White-backed Vulture (*G. bengalensis*), 30 inches (a similar bird but darker), generally live in large numbers in countries where food is very plentiful. The former are the vultures one normally sees assembling around carcases in large numbers in films of African game country. Always nesting in trees, they lay only one egg. Large vultures are often quite noisy, particularly when at carcases, uttering hisses, squeals and roars.

The Hooded Vulture (*Necrosyrtes monachus*), 24 to 26 inches, is found in Africa (excluding the Congo, the north and rarely in the extreme south). It visits carcases after the large vultures have eaten and gleans any small scraps left on the bones. Otherwise its feeding habits are crow-like, scavenging almost anywhere for small dead creatures or for garbage and so on. It lays one egg in nests in trees or cliff ledges.

The Egyptian Vulture (*Neophron percnopterus*), 21 to 26 inches, occurs over southern Europe, most of Africa, and across to India. It is similar in habits to the Hooded Vulture and both birds weigh about 4 pounds, compared with the 10 to 20 pounds of the larger vultures. Egyptian Vultures have a stronger foot and are able to kill slow-moving small reptiles and mammals, but they usually scavenge for carrion and refuse. They nest in a hole in a cliff, occasionally in trees or buildings, and lay two eggs.

The Lammergeyer (*Gypaetus barbatus*), 37 to 46 inches, is found in remote mountain areas of southern Europe, northern, eastern and southern Africa, and south-western and central Asia. It feeds on bones and carrion. It flies off with bones in its foot and drops them onto rocks to shatter them, afterwards alighting to eat the marrow and bone fragments. It has been seen to knock animals over cliff ledges or off scree slopes, but it has weak feet and cannot kill prey by other methods. It lays two eggs in a cave nest in a high cliff face.

Egyptian Vulture

Harriers

Harriers are found in open country throughout almost all the world except in the very cold regions and on some islands. The Spotted Harrier (*Circus assimilis*), 19 to 24 inches, found from Australia to Celebes, is brown spotted with white. The Long-winged Harrier (*C. buffoni*), 19 to 23 inches, of South America is black above and on the chest, and white or black below. The Black Harrier (*C. maurus*), 19 to 22 inches, of South Africa is blackish-brown with a white rump. The slightly smaller African Marsh Harrier (*C. ranivorus*), 18 to 20 inches, of southern and eastern Africa is nearly as dark, but the male has silver-grey on the wings, and both sexes have a barred tail. The Marsh Harrier (*C. aeruginosus*), 19 to 23 inches, is found over most of Europe, North Africa, central Asia, Madagascar, Australia and nearby islands, and New Zealand. The European male is illustrated but the plumage of both sexes is very variable.

In the next five species the females are brown above with a whitish rump, lighter below with dark streaks. The Pied Harrier (*C. melanoleucus*) is 18 to 20 inches long. The male is

African Harrier Hawk (*right*)
Marsh Harrier (*below*)

Hen Harrier

black on the head, back and wing tips, and whitish elsewhere. The Hen Harrier (*C. cyaneus*), 18 to 22 inches, is found over most of Europe, Asia and North America. It is grey above and on the head and chest, and white below. The Cinereous Harrier (*C. cinereus*), 18 to 20 inches, of southern and western South America is similar but banded orange-brown below. The Pallid Harrier (*C. macrourus*), 17 to 20 inches, found from eastern Europe to central Asia is pale grey above and white below. Montagu's Harrier (*C. pygargus*), 16 to 18 inches, found from western Europe to central Asia, is darker grey above with a black bar on the wings. It is streaked brown below. This last species is distinctly smaller than the others.

Harriers hunt mostly by flying low over moors, fields, marshes, and so on, surprising water birds, small land birds, rodents, reptiles, and frogs before they can fly off or run for cover. They lay three to six eggs in ground nests, except the Spotted Harrier which nests in trees.

The Crane Hawk (*Geranospiza caerulescens*), 16 to 20 inches, of central and South America is black or grey, the grey ones having white bars below. The African Harrier Hawk (*Polyboroides typus*), 20 to 27 inches, and the Madagascar Harrier Hawk (*P. radiatus*), 23 to 24 inches, which is clear grey on the head and chest, are similar in that they have double-jointed legs – an adaptation for reaching into holes in trees and on the ground for lizards and other small prey. The Crane Hawk lays one or two eggs in a tree nest; harrier hawks lay two eggs in a tree nest or on the ground in Madagascar.

Eurasian Short-toed Eagle with
Grass Snake

Snake Eagles

The Short-toed Eagle (*Circaetus gallicus*), 26 to 32 inches, is
found over southern Europe, most of Africa, southern and
central Asia. Southern Saharan birds are more finely barred
below. Eastern and southern African birds are blackish above
and on the chest, white below. The Brown Harrier Eagle
(*C. cinereus*), 29 to 31 inches, of Africa south of the Sahara, has
a heavier build and is dark brown. The Banded Harrier Eagle
(*C. cinerascens*), 25 to 26 inches, is found over much of Africa
south of the Sahara, except in the extreme south. It is not unlike
the Short-toed Eagle but has a black tail with a broad white
band. The Southern Banded Harrier Eagle (*C. fasciolatus*), 23
to 24 inches, of the eastern African coast is light below,
barred brown, and has three black bars on the tail.

The Crested Serpent Eagle (*Spilornis cheela*), 16 to 30 inches,
is found from northern India and China – where the largest
members of the species occur – to Borneo. The Philippine
Serpent Eagle (*S. holospilus*), 23 to 25 inches, is heavily spotted
above. The Celebes Serpent Eagle (*S. rufipectus*), 16 to 19
inches, is very dark with a rufous chest and is banded dark
brown below. The Nicobar Serpent Eagle (*S. klossi*), 15 to 16

inches, from Great Nicobar Island is very pale in colour and buffish below. The Andaman Serpent Eagle (*S. elgini*), 21 inches, is a rufous-brown bird, heavily spotted below.

The Gold Coast Serpent Eagle (*Dryotriorchis spectabilis*), 22 to 23 inches, of western Africa and the Congo forests is a short-winged, long-tailed bird. The Madagascar Serpent Eagle (*Eutriorchis astur*), 23 to 26 inches, has an even longer tail and is white, narrowly banded with black below. The Bateleur (*Terathopius ecaudatus*), 22 to 25 inches, is found in open country in Africa south of the Sahara (see page 32).

All these birds eat snakes and lizards. The Bateleur also eats a lot of carrion and kills small mammals. It flies up to 200 miles a day in search of food. The Short-toed Eagle also hunts open country, often hovering while searching the grass for snakes. All the other species do a great deal of still hunting and will take birds and small mammals occasionally. Most species are rather noisy, uttering loud caws and mewing whistles. Most lay one egg in a small nest in a tree.

Crested Serpent Eagle (*left*)
Gold Coast Serpent Eagle (*right*)

Pale Chanting Goshawk

Goshawks and Sparrow Hawks

Doria's Goshawk (*Megatriorchis doriae*), 23 to 27 inches, of New Guinea is brownish-black above, and white with short brown streaks below. It has very short wings and a long tail with twelve bars. The Red Goshawk (*Erythrotriorchis radiatus*), 20 to 23 inches, of northern and eastern Australia, is related to it. Both haunt wooded country hunting medium-sized birds, small mammals and snakes. They build large tree nests.

The Long-tailed Hawk (*Urotriorchis macrourus*), 24 inches, found in forests from Ghana to the Congo, catches birds and squirrels in the tree tops, but will also stalk birds on the ground.

The Dark Chanting Goshawk (*Melierax metabates*),

Red Goshawk

Long-tailed Hawk

17 to 20 inches, is found over most of Africa and southern Arabia. The Pale Chanting Goshawk (*M. canorus*), 18 to 21 inches, from eastern and southern Africa, differs from the previous bird in its white rump. Both inhabit dry, open bush country, usually still hunting from posts, bushes or rocks. They also hunt low like harriers, feeding mostly on lizards. They nest in bushes or trees, laying one egg, sometimes two. The Gabar Goshawk (*M. gabar*), 11 to 14 inches, is like the previous species in colour or all black. It inhabits more wooded country, where it pursues small birds and builds a tree nest.

The Northern Goshawk (*Accipiter gentilis*), is found throughout northern temperate regions. The Black and White Goshawk (*A. melanoleucus*) of southern Africa, Henst's Goshawk (*A. hensti*) of Madagascar, Bürger's Goshawk (*A. buergersi*) of New Guinea, and Meyer's Goshawk (*A. meyerianus*) from nearby islands are all large (17 to 24 inches), closely related Goshawks. They are brown, grey or black above, and white – usually streaked or barred dark – below. They still hunt or kill after a quick dash.

Gundlach's Hawk (*A. gundlachi*), 16 to 19 inches, a rare bird from Cuba, is bluish above, and barred brown below. Cooper's Hawk (*A. cooperii*) of southern Canada south to Mexico is similar and preys more on birds. From Mexico southwards, the Bi-coloured Hawk (*A. bicolor*) occurs. The tropical birds are smaller (13 to 15 inches), usually grey below with rufous thighs. Southern birds resemble Cooper's Hawk. The rare Grey-bellied Goshawk (*A. poliogaster*), 17 to 19 inches, of

Northern Goshawk (American race)

tropical South America is dark grey above, grey-white below.

Small lightly-built hawks with long toes, which enable them to grasp fast-moving small birds, are found throughout the world except the very cold regions. The Sharp-shinned Hawk (*A. striatus*) of the New World is similar in colour to Cooper's Hawk in North America, but very variable farther south. The Tiny Hawk (*A. superciliosus*), 9 to 12 inches, is found in tropical South America. The Eurasian Sparrow Hawk (*A. nisus*), 11 to 15 inches, is brown above and white barred with brown below. Males are brighter than females. The Madagascar Sparrow Hawk (*A. madagascariensis*) is similar to the Eurasian female, as is the Ovampo Sparrow Hawk (*A. ovampensis*), 9 to 11 inches, which inhabits open country in southern Africa. In eastern and southern Africa the Rufous-breasted Sparrow Hawk (*A. rufiventris*) is its forest equivalent. In Japan, the Lesser Sparrow Hawk (*A. gularis*), 9 to 12 inches, is rather like the Eurasian species. Throughout south-eastern Asia the brighter coloured Besra Sparrow Hawk (*A. virgatus*), 9 to 12 inches, occurs. In Celebes, the Celebes Little Sparrow Hawk (*A. nanus*), 9 to 11 inches, occurs in lowland forest, and the Vinous-breasted Sparrow Hawk (*A. rhodogaster*), 11 to 13 inches, in the hills. Throughout the Moluccas the Grey-throated Sparrow Hawk (*A. erythrauchen*), 11 to 14 inches, lives. The similar but shorter-tailed New Britain Sparrow

Hawk (*A. brachyurus*), 11 to 13 inches, is intermediate in appearance between the Grey-throated and the Collared Sparrow Hawk (*A. cirrhocephalus*), 10 to 13 inches, of Australia and New Guinea. In Venezuela, Colombia, and Ecuador, the rare Semi-collared Sparrow Hawk (*A. collaris*), 11 to 12 inches, is very local. Africa south of the Sahara has two small species, the Little Sparrow Hawk (*A. minullus*), 9 to 11 inches, and the Western Little Sparrow Hawk (*A. erythropus*), 9 to 11 inches, of the West African forests.

The following species have a heavier build and stronger, shorter legs and toes. The African Goshawk (*A. tachiro*), 14 to 17 inches, is blackish above with chestnut barring below. The Chestnut-sided Goshawk (*A. castanilius*), 11 to 14 inches, occurs in tropical West Africa. The Grey-headed Goshawk (*A. poliocephalus*), 13 to 15 inches, is found on islands west of New Guinea. The New Britain Grey-headed Goshawk (*A. princeps*) is similar but larger. The Spot-tailed Goshawk (*A. trinotatus*), 12 inches, of Celebes is vinous below. The Chinese Goshawk (*A. soloensis*), 10 to 12 inches, is grey above, reddish or white below. The Shikra (*A. badius*), 11 to 14 inches, grey above, barred brown or rufous below, is found in southern Asia and Africa. The Nicobar Shikra (*A. butleri*), 11 to 13

Three phases of Grey or
Variable Goshawk

Rufous-breasted Sparrow
Hawk chasing Wheatear

inches, is paler above and more rufous below. The Levant
Sparrow Hawk (*A. brevipes*), 13 to 15 inches, of the Black Sea
region, is darker above. Frances's Sparrow Hawk (*A. francesii*),
11 to 13 inches, of Madagascar has faint grey bars below.

The Crested Goshawk (*A. trivirgatus*), 13 to 18 inches,
found from India to Borneo, is grey above and has a black
streak on its white throat. The Celebes Crested Goshawk
(*A. griseiceps*), 13 to 15 inches, has a blue head and white
underparts streaked with dark. The Black-mantled Goshawk
(*A. melanochlamys*), 13 to 15 inches, black above and reddish-
brown below, occurs in New Guinea. Closely related are the
Pied Goshawk (*A. albogularis*), 13 to 16 inches, of the
Solomons, the Black-throated Goshawk (*A. haplochrous*), 14 to
16 inches, of New Caledonia, and the Fiji Goshawk (*A.
rufitorques*), 13 to 16 inches, which is light grey above and
reddish below and on its collar. Also on the Solomons is the
Imitator Hawk (*A. imitator*), 11 to 13 inches, which superficially resembles the Pied Goshawk but is unrelated. On New
Britain, the Blue and Grey Sparrow Hawk (*A. luteoschistaceus*),
12 to 15 inches, has a slaty back and buffish underparts.
The Moluccan species, Gray's Goshawk (*A. henicogrammus*),
15 to 19 inches, is dark grey above, and chestnut barred
white below. The White, Grey or Vinous Goshawk (*A. novae-*

Far right Lizard Buzzard (*above*)
White-eyed Buzzard (*below*)

hollandiae), 13 to 20 inches, occurs in Australia, New Guinea and nearby islands. The Grey-throated Goshawk (*A. griseogularis*), 17 to 19 inches, occurs in the Moluccas. The Australian Goshawk (*A. fasciatus*), 13 to 20 inches, occurs from Christmas Island and Java to New Caledonia.

All Accipiters almost invariably build a nest in a tree. The clutch varies from two to six eggs in different species.

The Lizard Buzzard (*Kaupifalco monogrammicus*), 12 to 13 inches, is found in Africa south of the Sahara, in open country with scattered trees. It hunts lizards, snakes, rodents, in some areas birds.

The Grasshopper Buzzard (*Butastur rufipennis*), 14 to 16 inches, found from Senegal to Somalia, is ginger-coloured. It feeds mostly on insects. The White-eyed Buzzard (*B. teesa*), 15 to 17 inches, from India and Burma, still hunts for insects, frogs and lizards. The Rufous-winged Buzzard (*B. liventer*), 15 to 17 inches, from Thailand, Malaysia and Indonesia, and the Grey-faced Buzzard (*B. indicus*), 16 to 18 inches, which is found in China and Japan in summer, are similar in habits. Butasturs usually nest in trees and lay three eggs.

Rough-legged Buzzard

Buzzards

The Buzzards tend to be less specialized than do other birds of prey. They are not as strong as some nor as fast as others, but nevertheless they are a very successful group and are found almost throughout the world. The Grey Hawk (*Buteo nitidus*), 15 to 17 inches, is grey with white barring below. It is found from Mexico to northern Argentina in fairly open country with scattered bushes and trees. It hunts in a hawk-like manner – dashing low after birds, small mammals, reptiles and insects. The Roadside Hawk (*B. magnirostris*), 11 to 14 inches, is a brownish bird, pale below with brown bars, from southern Mexico to northern Argentina. Its very similar close relatives, Ridgway's Hawk (*B. ridgwayi*) of Hispaniola and the White-rumped hawk (*B. leucorrhous*), 14 to 15 inches, a mainly black bird found from western South America to southern Brazil, are also still hunters. The Broad-winged Hawk (*B. platypterus*), 14 to 18 inches, of the United States and certain Caribbean Islands is brown above and grey or brown below spotted and barred with white. This bird and the Red-shouldered Hawk (*B. lineatus*), 16 to 20 inches, of the United States, a rufous bird with a distinctly barred blackish and white tail, both live in wooded or swampy country. They eat fish and amphibians in addition to usual buzzard's fare. The Short-tailed Hawk (*B. brachyurus*), 15 to 17 inches, which is dark above and white below or all dark, is found from Florida to the southern Andes. The mountain forms are streaked with brown.

The Red-backed Buzzard (*B. polyosoma*), 19 to 21 inches,

Red-tailed Buzzard binding to North American Cacomistle

Common Buzzard

and Gurney's Buzzard (*B. poecilochrous*), 20 to 22 inches, both have several colour phases. Females have brick-red backs, grey wings and may be light with fine barring, or dark below. Males may be grey or black above and below, or white below, sometimes with some red on the back. Both species are Andean birds but Gurney's Buzzard, which has longer wings, is found only north of Chile and at high altitudes. The White-tailed Buzzard (*B. albicaudatus*), 23 to 24 inches, is a long-winged bird found in open country from the southern United States to Argentina. It has reddish-brown shoulders and may be light or dark below with a broad, black subterminal band on the tail. It lives mostly on lizards and rodents. These

White-tailed Buzzard

buzzards are attracted to grass or cane fires and they circle overhead on the look out for prey seeking to escape the flames.

A huge buzzard from South America, the Grey Eagle Buzzard (*B. melanoleucus*), 22 to 31 inches, is grey above and on the breast. Birds from the Andes are white, finely barred with grey below, whereas birds from low regions south of Paraguay are completely white underneath. It has very long wings and a short wedge-shaped tail, making its flight silhouette resemble that of a sea eagle. The Ferruginous Rough-legged Buzzard (*B. regalis*), 24 to 26 inches, from the western United States and southern Canada is brown or rufous above and white below or all blackish. The Rough-legged Buzzard (*B. lagopus*), 20 to 24 inches, is a variable bird which generally has much white on the head, chest and tail. It is found over most low arctic regions. The last two species have legs feathered to the toes and live mainly on rodents. The Long-legged Buzzard (*B. rufinus*), 22 to 26 inches, is a variable brown bird with a rufous-brown tail found from North Africa to central Asia. The Upland Buzzard (*B. hemilasius*), 24 to 27 inches, of central Asia is rather similar but has completely feathered legs. Both species are powerful birds capable of killing animals up to the size of a hare.

The Red-tailed Buzzard (*B. jamaicensis*), 20 to 23 inches,

of North America, the Common and Steppe Buzzard (*B. buteo*), 19 to 22 inches, of Europe and Asia, and the South American Red-tailed Buzzard (*B. ventralis*), 19 to 21 inches, of Patagonia, all inhabit hilly and wooded areas in temperate regions.

Grey Hawk

shade from blackish-brown to buff. The tails are usually red or brown with darker bars. The Mountain Buzzard (*B. oreophilus*), 16 to 18 inches, found above 6,000 feet in eastern and southern Africa, is dark above, white marked with brown on the breast, and rufous below. The Madagascar Buzzard (*B. brachypterus*), 16 to 18 inches, is similar but has more white below and rather short wings. Swainson's Buzzard (*B. swainsoni*), 18 to 21 inches, of western North America, has a brown breast and is buff with dark bars below, or is all dark. Both phases have a grey tail barred with brown.

Two buzzards are found on Pacific islands. The Galapagos Buzzard (*B. galapagoensis*), 19 to 22 inches, is a mainly dark brown bird which is the tamest of the world's birds of prey. The Hawaiian Buzzard (*B. solitarius*), 15 to 17 inches, is

Roadside Hawk
with anole lizard

Harris' Hawk

dark above and white on the head and below with buff or sometimes brown marks. There is also a dark brown phase.

The African Red-tailed Buzzard (*B. auguralis*), 16 to 18 inches, occurs over most of West Africa and the Sudan. It is usually brown above, on the head, and on the breast, and whitish with dark marks below. In eastern and southern Africa, the Augur Buzzard (*B. rufofuscus*), 19 to 22 inches, is a large buzzard with a short rufous tail. It is usually black or grey above and may be white, rufous or black below. In central and northern South America, the Zone-tailed Buzzard (*B. albonotatus*), 18 to 21 inches, is a blackish bird with wide white bars on the tail.

Most buzzards spend much time soaring, but they usually still hunt or they may fly harrier- or hawk-fashion in search of prey which consists mostly of mammals up to rabbit size. Some also hover when hunting open country or even walk about on the ground. Most species are noisy. They generally nest in a tree, but in hilly country, often use a rock ledge.

Harris' Hawk (*Parabuteo unicinctus*), 19 to 22 inches, is a reddish-brown and dark brown bird with powerful legs and feet. It occurs from the south-western United States to

Black-faced Hawk (*behind*)   White Hawk (*front*)

southern South America, living in dry bush country where it hunts in a hawk-like manner for birds and mammals up to the size of small herons and rabbits. It lays three to five eggs.

The Savannah Hawk (*Heterospizias meridionalis*) grows 20 to 24 inches long. This long-legged South American bird feeds mostly on snakes and lizards, which it generally hunts from a perch a few feet from the ground. Its colour is bright reddish and grey-brown. The one or two eggs are laid in a tree nest.

The following birds are tropical buzzards, inhabiting forests and isolated groups of trees in low open country in South and Central America. The Slate-coloured Hawk (*Leucopternis schistacea*), 17 to 18 inches, has brown on the wings and a black tail with a white band and white tip. It lives in Colombia, Venezuela, and northern Brazil. The Plumbeous Hawk (*L. plumbea*), 15 inches, of western Colombia and Ecuador is also slate grey with black wings and a black tail which has a white band. The Semi-plumbeous Hawk (*L. semiplumbea*) of Central America and western Colombia is 15 inches in size and similar to the Plumbeous Hawk, but is white below. The White-browed Hawk (*L. kuhli*) of the Amazon is 15 inches in size and is dark above and white on the brow, sides of the neck and below. The Black-faced Hawk (*L. melanops*), from the Guianas to the Amazon, is 16 inches in size.

The Mantled Hawk (*L. polionota*), 19 to 21 inches, of southern Brazil and Paraguay is black above and on the upper half of the tail and white everywhere else. The White Hawk (*L. albicollis*), 19 to 23 inches, found from Mexico to Bolivia, is white with black on the wings and tail band. The Grey-backed Hawk (*L. occidentalis*), 19 inches, of western Ecuador is white below, streaked dark on the sides with a black band on the lower tail. And the Barred Hawk (*L. princeps),* 18 to 20 inches, is a black bird with finely barred underparts which inhabits mountain forests from Costa Rica to Ecuador. These hawks are mostly still hunters but are able to move quickly among the branches of forest trees in pursuit of lizards, snakes, small mammals and slow-moving birds.

The Black-collared Fishing Hawk (*Busarellus nigricollis*), 19 to 21 inches, is found from Mexico to northern Argentina, generally in low-lying country subject to flooding. The undersides of the toes are furnished with spike-like scales similar to the Osprey's, and this bird lives mostly by snatching fish from the surface of the water. It will also eat crabs, small mammals and reptiles. It builds its nest in a tall tree.

Crowned Harpy Eagle

The Rufous Crab Hawk (*Buteogallus aequinoctialis*), 16 to 19 inches in size and found in coastal swamp forests of northern and eastern South America, is a reddish-brown bird with some grey on the head and wings. It eats mainly crabs but will take frogs and fish. The Common Black Hawk (*B. anthracinus*), 18 to 23 inches, is generally found in wooded areas near water from the southern United States to northern South America. It is similar to the Great Black Hawk but has some brown mottling on the wings and white near the wing tips. The Great Black Hawk (*B. urubitinga*), 20 to 25 inches, found from southern Mexico to northern Argentina, inhabits similar areas but is sometimes found in dry regions. Both catch fish, frogs, lizards and snakes. The Great Black Hawk also takes small mammals and birds, the Common Black Hawk seldom does. Buteogallus nests in trees and lays one or two eggs.

The Solitary Eagle (*Harpyhaliaetus solitarius*), 27 to 29 inches, is a dark brown bird with a short crest, and a black tail with a white bar and tip. It is found from Mexico along the Andes to Peru. The Crowned Eagle (*H. coronatus*), 29 to 32 inches, a much greyer bird with a long crest, replaces the Solitary Eagle from Bolivia to Argentina. Both species catch mammals up to the size of young deer and even kill skunks.

Great Black Hawk

Black-collared
Fishing Hawk

Harpy Eagle with Agouti

Harpy Eagles

The Crested Eagle (*Morphnus guianensis*), 32 to 36 inches, inhabits tropical forests from Honduras to northern Argentina. A rather slim, long-tailed, long-legged eagle, this bird is brownish-black above, grey or black on the chest, and white barred with rufous or black below. Its tail is black with ashy-brown bars. This eagle preys mainly on mammals up to the size of a small monkey and often kills reptiles. It nests high up in huge forest trees and probably lays only one egg.

The Harpy Eagle (*Harpia harpyja*) grows 36 to 40 inches long. An average female is the world's most powerful eagle, the hind claws being thicker – but not quite as long – as those of the largest carnivore, the Kodiak Bear. It inhabits tropical forests from southern Mexico to northern Argentina. Unlike the previous species, the Harpy seldom soars. A female may weigh 18 pounds and can lift heavy prey almost vertically with the aid of its rather short, broad wings. It kills monkeys, sloths, and even small peccaries and any large forest birds, including macaws. It often nests in the largest tree in the vicinity, and

Monkey-eating Eagle

lays one egg as far as is known so far to ornithologists.

The New Guinea Harpy Eagle (*Harpyopsis novaeguineae*) grows 30 to 34 inches long. Another large forest eagle, it resembles a Monkey-eating Eagle but has shorter beak and slimmer legs and toes. It often has orange-buff markings below. It preys on marsupial mammals and has been known to kill pigs. Its nesting habits are similar to those of the previous species.

The Monkey-eating Eagle (*Pithecophaga jefferyi*) of the Philippine Islands is 34 to 40 inches in size and is now found only on Mindanao and Luzon. It is the rarest eagle in the world and there are probably not more than fifty pairs surviving today. Almost as powerful as the Harpy, this huge forest eagle is known to kill monkeys and also large forest birds including hornbills. It has a loud plaintive call which it often uses. It is more prolific than other large forest eagles, laying two eggs and apparently breeding most years. It chooses the usual nest site of forest eagles, a tall tree.

True Eagles

With one or two exceptions, all the birds described so far have the lower parts of their legs covered by scales. The following species, the true eagles, are all feathered to the toes.

The Lesser Spotted Eagle (*Aquila pomarina*) of eastern Europe, south-eastern Asia and India is 24 to 26 inches in size and is a lightly built, long-winged brown eagle which gets its name from the fact that the young bird has two rows of white spots on the wings. The young of the Greater Spotted Eagle (*A. clanga*), 26 to 29 inches, is even more heavily spotted but the adult is dark brown, generally with a white rump. It has a heavier build than has the Lesser Spotted, with a much broader wing tip when seen in flight. Both birds are woodland species, often (especially the latter) found near water. They prey on small mammals, reptiles, frogs, water birds, and so on.

The Tawny Eagle (*A. rapax*) of Africa and Asia is 26 to 31 inches in size and is the world's commonest eagle. It may be almost any shade of brown. Birds found in central Asia and eastern Europe are larger and known as Steppe Eagles. They take a wide variety of prey from eagle owls to flying ants, and they also eat carrion. They nest in trees, or sometimes on the ground or on rock ledges. They lay one or two eggs, occasionally three. The Imperial Eagle (*A. heliaca*), 31 to 33 inches, from the Iberian peninsula, eastern Europe and central Asia, has white patches on the upper back; western birds have white shoulders. It usually lays two eggs in tree nests.

Spanish Imperial Eagle with
Red Squirrel

Wedge-tailed Eagle *(left)*
(Below) Golden Eagle in flight seen from below

The Golden Eagle (*A. chrysaetos*), 30 to 40 inches, is found in mountainous regions throughout the northern hemisphere. It may be any shade of brown, but is generally golden on the hind neck. Golden Eagles are very powerful birds; the largest in Asia regularly kill wolves and they have been known to kill fairly large deer. They are fast enough to catch many kinds of large birds, but their most general prey is mammals up to the size of a hare. They build huge nests on trees or rock ledges. Eggs are usually two, occasionally one or three. Verreaux's Eagle (*A. verreauxi*), 32 to 35 inches, is a black eagle with a white back. It lives on mountains in eastern and southern Africa, and preys almost exclusively on the Rock Hyrax. It generally lays its one or two eggs in a nest on a crag. The Wedge-tailed Eagle (*A. audax*), 34 to 40 inches, of Australia and Tasmania (where largest birds occur) is a blackish and brown eagle preying mostly on mammals up to the size of small kangaroos. It also eats reptiles and carrion. It will drive prey from cover by dropping sticks onto it. Two eggs are laid in large tree nests. Gurney's Eagle (*A. gurneyi*), 26 to 30 inches, of western New Guinea is blackish with short wings and long tail.

Black Eagle with bird's nest

Black Eagle and Forest Hawk Eagles

The Indian Black Eagle (*Ictinaetus malayensis*), 25 to 29 inches, inhabits jungle, especially on hills, from the Himalayas to Celebes. A lightly-built bird with very long wings and tail, it is a most buoyant flier, gliding even in unfavourable weather conditions with scarcely a wing flap. It glides down to tree-top level and snatches nests from the branches, eating both eggs and young birds. It also catches lizards and birds up to the size of small pheasants, as well as small mammals. It builds a large tree nest and usually lays only one egg.

The Mountain Hawk Eagle (*Spizaetus nipalensis*), 26 to 34 inches, is found from Ceylon through southern India and the Himalayas to as far north as Japan, where the largest individuals occur. Short-winged, long-tailed forest birds, they are brown above and fawn below with white bars. Some have long crests. They are still hunters which prey on small mammals, young monkeys and young small deer. They lay one egg in a nest in a forest tree. The Java Hawk Eagle (*S. bartelsi*), 22 to 24 inches, is a blackish bird with a brownish band across the tail and white barring below. Little is known about it. The Celebes Hawk Eagle (*S. lanceolatus*), 22 to 25 inches, is black and brown above, rufous with black streaks on the chest, and

Ornate Hawk Eagle

barred brown and white below. It has a very short crest. The
Philippine Hawk Eagle (*S. philippensis*), 25 to 27 inches, is
similar but has brown underparts. Blyth's Hawk Eagle (*S.
alboniger*), 20 to 23 inches, found from southern Burma to
Sumatra and Borneo, is brownish-black above and white
below. It is streaked on the breast and barred below with
black, has a whitish band on the tail and a long crest. It
inhabits almost the same area as does Wallace's Hawk Eagle
(*S. nanus*), 18 to 20 inches, which is brown above, with head
and underparts pinkish-buff, sometimes with dark markings.
The Changeable Hawk Eagle (*S. cirrhatus*), 22 to 32 inches,
occurs from northern India to Mindanao and Flores, where the
largest specimens occur. It may be all blackish or dark above
and white below, or the underparts may be streaked or all
brown. Crests may be present – as in most Indian birds – or
absent, as in most parts of its range. It sits very still in an erect
position with its feathers drawn in tight and on sighting prey
(usually lizards, medium-sized birds or small mammals) it
makes a sudden quick dash at it. Its nesting habits are like
those of the Mountain Hawk Eagle. Both species have an
unusual call consisting of a series of shrill piping notes.

Martial Eagle striking at guinea fowl

Large Forest Eagles

Cassin's Hawk Eagle (*S. africanus*) of western Africa and the Congo forests is 22 to 24 inches in size and is black above, white below, and has no crest. It catches arboreal animals such as squirrels, and medium-sized birds. Little else is known about it. The Tyrant or Black Hawk Eagle (*S. tyrannus*), 25 to 28 inches, is found in lowland forests from southern Mexico to northern Argentina. It is brownish-black with a long grey barred tail and white markings on the crest and underparts. The Ornate Hawk Eagle (*S. ornatus*), 24 to 26 inches, is found throughout the same area. It probably attacks small mammals and lizards and kills fewer birds than does the Tyrant Hawk Eagle. It frequently soars with wings held flat. As with all crested eagles, the position of the long crest indicates the mood or disposition of the bird. The Ornate Hawk Eagle breeds in giant forest trees and lays one egg.

The Crowned Hawk Eagle (*Stephanoaetus coronatus*), 32 to 39 inches, is found in forest regions and in fairly well wooded areas in Africa south of the Sahara. One of the world's most powerful eagles, it preys on small antelopes, monkeys, hyraxes, ground birds, and occasionally on snakes and lizards. It is less of a still hunter than are most hawk eagles, often flying slowly and quietly among the trees. Like the Harpy Eagle, which has similar proportions, it can lift heavy prey almost vertically from the ground to a branch above. It generally lays two eggs in a huge nest in a tall tree. The beautiful repetitive two-note piping call is the finest of all the birds of prey. It also utters a loud call during display.

The Black and Chestnut Eagle (*Oroaetus isidori*), 25 to 29 inches, is black above and on its long crest, head and thighs. It is reddish-brown below and has a grey tail with a broad black tip. It inhabits mountain forests in western South America from Venezuela to Argentina. It hunts monkeys, squirrels and other small to medium-sized animals, apparently even killing porcupines. It lays one egg in a nest in a tree, usually one growing on a precipitous slope.

The Martial Eagle (*Polemaetus bellicosus*), 32 to 38 inches, is a long-winged, short-crested species inhabiting savannah and open wooded country in Africa south of the Sahara. It has long legs and toes, adaptations for clutching medium-sized birds such as francolins or guinea fowl in flight. It often spots prey while soaring high in the air, then sets off on a long fast glide towards it. Indeed, it spends a good deal of time on the wing, and when not hunting frequently soars for hours very high up in the sky. It also kills small antelopes, hyraxes and takes poultry and goats. It builds a large nest in a tree, and lays only one egg.

Crowned Hawk Eagle

87

Bonelli's Eagle *or* African Hawk Eagle

Hawk Eagles

The Long-crested Hawk Eagle (*Lophoaetus occipitalis*), 20 to 22 inches, is found in Africa south of the Sahara in farmlands, lightly-forested areas, and grassland with scattered trees. It is fairly tame and still hunts for rodents, reptiles and insects. It nests in a tree, and lays one or two eggs.

The Black and White Hawk Eagle (*Spizastur melanoleucus*), 21 to 24 inches, is black above and on the crest, and white on the head and below. It inhabits forests from southern Mexico to Argentina, preying on small mammals, birds and reptiles.

The Booted Eagle (*Hieraaetus pennatus*), 19 to 25 inches, may be all brown or brown above and light below. It inhabits open forests, often in dry, rocky or hill country in southern Europe and northern Africa, extending to central Asia and India. It often nests in small trees. The Little Eagle (*H.*

morphnoides) of New Guinea and Australia is 17 to 22 inches in size and is similar to the Booted Eagle but has a more pronounced crest which, with the top of the head, is blackish in colour. It takes more mammals than does the Booted Eagle and also kills reptiles. Ayres' Hawk Eagle (*H. dubius*), 19 to 21 inches, is found from Togo and Ethiopia to South Africa. It is dark brown above and white with dark marks below. It catches birds and squirrels. Bonelli's or African Hawk Eagle (*H. fasciatus*), 26 to 31 inches, is found in southern Europe, southern Asia, the island of Flores and most of Africa. It inhabits rocky hills in dry areas. It is able to catch large birds and mammals up to the size of small antelopes. It nests on rock ledges or in trees; two eggs are usual. The Rufous-bellied Hawk Eagle (*H. kienerii*), 19 to 24 inches, is black above, white on the throat and breast, and reddish below. It is found from southern and eastern India to Celebes. Wahlberg's Eagle (*H. wahlbergi*), 22 to 24 inches, is a long-winged eagle, which is all brown, or brown above and light below. Found over most of Africa south of the Sahara, it is not a strong bird.

Laughing Falcon with
Coral Snake

Forest Falcons

The Laughing Falcon (*Herpetotheres cachinnans*), 17 to 20
inches, is found from Mexico to Argentina, occurring in both
forests and in dry open country – anywhere where snakes,
their main prey, are numerous. Unlike most falcons, these are
short-winged birds with fairly long tails. They are normally
still hunters and are noisy birds, especially in the evening.
They lay one egg in a hole in a tree or cliff, or occasionally in
an old nest of another bird of prey.

The Collared Forest Falcon (*Micrastur semitorquatus*), 18 to
24 inches, is also found from Mexico to Argentina. A short-
winged, long-tailed bird, it is not a strong flier but is able to
glide rapidly through forest trees and to move quickly both
among the branches and on the ground. It catches fairly large
birds, often larger than itself. Traylor's Forest Falcon (*M.
buckleyi*) from Ecuador is 16 to 18 inches in size and similar to
the Collared Forest Falcon but has brown centres to the tail
feathers. It is comparatively smaller with much smaller legs
and feet. Little is known about it. The Slaty-backed Forest
Falcon (*M. mirandollei*), found from Costa Rica to Peru and
the mouth of the Amazon, is 17 to 18 inches in size and is also

similar to the Collared Forest Falcon but has a slate-grey back and no white collar. The Barred Forest Falcon (*M. ruficollis*), 12 to 15 inches, is found from Mexico to Argentina in mountains and lowland forests. A very variable species, it is usually closely barred white and blackish below and grey, reddish or almost any shade of brown above. The tail generally has three white bars above in the female, two in the male. The Plumbeous Forest Falcon (*M. plumbeus*), 12 to 14 inches, from Ecuador and south-western Colombia, is similar to the Barred Forest Falcon but has only one tail band. Nothing is known of the breeding habits of forest falcons except that some nest in tall trees.

The Yellow-throated Caracara (*Daptrius ater*), 16 to 18 inches, is a greenish-black bird with a white band across the tail and bare yellow skin on the face. It occurs in the forests of the Amazon and its tributaries. The Red-throated Caracara (*D. americanus*), 16 to 24 inches, occurs in forests from southern Mexico to southern Brazil, where the largest members of the species occur. It is black above and on the breast, white below. The bare skin on the face and throat is red. Both species

91

Common Caracara

eat fruit and catch mostly insects, raiding wasps nests and catching large beetles, but they also kill small vertebrates that are not difficult to catch. They nest in high forest trees and lay two to three eggs.

Carrion Hawks

The Carunculated Caracara (*Phalcoboenus carunculatus*), 19 to 21 inches, is a black bird with white streaking below and white on the rump, vent and tail-tip. It has a bare orange or red throat and face, which is very wrinkled. It is found in Colombia and Ecuador. The Mountain Caracara (*P. megalopterus*) of Peru, Bolivia and northern Chile is 19 to 21 inches in size and has a black breast and white underparts. The White-throated Caracara (*P. albogularis*) of Chile and Argentina is 19 to 21 inches in size and is entirely white below. Forster's Caracara (*P. australis*) of the Falkland Islands and islands near Tierra del Fuego is 23 to 25 inches in size and black with fine white streaks, rufous on the abdomen and thighs. These four closely-related birds are found in the Andes in high treeless

Forster's Caracara

Red-throated Caracara

areas, or in the case of Forster's Caracara in similar areas near the sea. They are sociable birds, feeding mostly on carrion and invertebrates. They breed on cliffs, laying two to four eggs.

The Chimango Caracara (*Milvago chimango*) of southern South America is 15 to 16 inches in size, rufous brown above, white on the rump and brown, mottled buffish-white below. From Panama to northern Argentina excepting the Andes, the Yellow-headed Caracara (*M. chimachima*), 15 to 18 inches, occurs. These two species frequent lightly wooded and open country, also sea shores. Usually seen pecking on the ground, they are omnivorous and have a similar diet to that of crows and rooks. The nests may be built in trees, bushes or on the ground. They usually lay three eggs.

The Common Caracara (*Polyborus plancus*), 20 to 26 inches, is found from the southern United States to Tierra del Fuego. A bird of open country which will eat almost anything, it spends much time on the ground where it can run rapidly, as can most carrion hawks. It is very noisy and has a loud rattling call. It may rob other birds of food and attacks birds up to its own size if they are injured or sick. It nests in trees and lays two or three eggs.

Yellow-headed Caracara

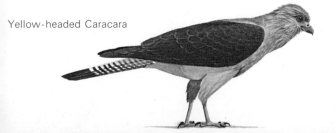

Spot-winged Falcon

Fielden's Falconet

94

Pygmy Falcons

The Spot-winged Falcon (*Spizapteryx circumcinctus*), 11 to 12 inches, is short-winged and inhabits open woodland in parts of northern Argentina. It is said to prey mainly on birds. Its nesting habits are unrecorded.

The Red-thighed Falconet or Pygmy Falcon (*Microhierax caerulescens*), 5½ to 6½ inches (see page 4), occurs from northern India to Vietnam. The Black-legged Falconet (*M. fringillarius*), 5½ to 6 inches, is black above and on the thighs, white on the chest and rufous below. It occurs from the Malay peninsula to Bali, and in southern Borneo. The Pied Falconet (*M. melanoleucus*), 6 to 7 inches, is black above and white on the forehead, eyestripe and below. It occurs from Assam to southern China. The White-headed or Bornean Falconet (*M. latifrons*) of northern Borneo, which is 6 inches in size, is illustrated on page 22. The Philippine Falconet (*M. erythrogonys*), 6 to 7 inches, is greenish-black above and on the thighs, and white below and on the sides of the neck and head. In spite of their small size, pygmy falcons can catch birds up to the size of a small thrush. They also take small mammals and large insects. They nest in holes in trees, laying three to four eggs.

Fielden's Falconet (*Poliohierax insignis*), 10 to 11 inches, has a longer, rounder tail than do other pygmy falcons, and the female has a red head. It is found from Burma to Cambodia. It builds a tree nest. The African Pygmy Falcon (*P. semitorquatus*), 7½ inches, found in dry areas in southern and eastern Africa, is grey above and white below. The female is chestnut on the back. Usually seen in pairs, these birds prey mostly on insects and lizards. They nest in the old nests of small birds.

The Brown Falcon (*Falco berigora*) of Australia and New Guinea, 15 to 18 inches, is very variable in colouring. It is generally common and still hunts more than most large falcons.

Kestrels

The White-eyed Kestrel (*F. rupicoloides*), 13 to 14 inches, of eastern and southern Africa is a brown, heavily barred bird confined to dry bush country with scattered trees. It is more of a still hunter than is the Common Kestrel because it is a less efficient flier. It lays three to five eggs in an old nest of another bird, most often that of a Cape Rook. The Fox Kestrel (*F.*

alopex), 14 to 15 inches, is found on rocky hills in dry country from Ghana to the Sudan and Ethiopia. It is a long-winged, long-tailed chestnut bird which feeds mainly on grasshoppers and small lizards. It nests in crevices in cliffs. The Common Kestrel (*F. tinnunculus*), 12 to 14 inches, is found over most of Europe, Africa and Asia, except in high Arctic, extreme desert and heavily forested regions. Because it is the expert at hovering flight it can exploit the rodent population of the open country and is therefore more successful than any other bird of prey. For the same reason, it is the most numerous species. It eats small birds, lizards, frogs, and worms. The male is illustrated. The female resembles the White-eyed Kestrel but has dark eyes. It nests in an old nest of large birds, or in hollow trees or on cliff ledges. It usually lays four or five eggs. The Madagascar Kestrel (*F. newtoni*), 10 to 11 inches, which also lives on the Comoro and Aldabra Islands, has the sexes similar but occurs in two colour phases. One is light rufous above streaked with black, and whitish below. The other is dark rufous above and below, heavily streaked with black. The Mauritius Kestrel (*F. punctatus*), 11 to 13 inches, now probably the rarest bird of prey, resembles a female Common Kestrel but is white below spotted with black or rufous. It has only six bars on the tail. The Seychelles Kestrel

Grey Kestrel

Common Kestrel

(*F. araea*), 9 to 10 inches, resembles a tiny male Common Kestrel but is unspotted below and has more bars on the tail. The Moluccan Kestrel (*F. moluccensis*), 11 to 13 inches, is a pale chestnut bird, heavily spotted and streaked with black throughout. Both sexes are similar except that the male has only one band on a blue-grey tail whereas the female has several. The Nankeen Kestrel (*F. cenchroides*), 11 to 12 inches, of Australia and the highlands of New Guinea resembles the Common Kestrel but both sexes tend to be amber-brown where the Common Kestrel is rufous-brown. In New Guinea, both sexes resemble male Common Kestrels. Behaviour and nesting habits are also similar to those of the Common Kestrel. The Lesser Kestrel (*F. naumanni*), 11 to 12 inches, is an insectivorous species found in southern Europe and central Asia in summer, migrating south in winter. Males resemble Common Kestrels but have unspotted red backs. Females resemble small female Common Kestrels, but both sexes have white claws. They catch much of their prey in the air, are very sociable and breed in colonies in cliffs and buildings.

American Kestrel hovering

The American Kestrel (*F. sparverius*), 9 to 12 inches, breeds from southern Alaska and Newfoundland, south to Patagonia. It is lightly built, like the Lesser Kestrel, but with more of the Common Kestrel's habits. Although it prefers an insect diet, it will take small rodents, birds, snakes and lizards. Females are banded reddish-brown and dark brown on the wings and tail. The male bird is illustrated on page 97. Nesting habits are the same as those of the Common Kestrel.

The Grey Kestrel (*F. ardosiaceus*), 13 to 14 inches, is found in open woodland in parts of western, central and eastern

Merlin hunting

Africa. A heavy, stocky kestrel and mainly a still hunter, it is said to feed mostly on insects but its strength and weight make this doubtful. It lays three to five eggs in a hole in trees or in an old nest. Dickinson's Kestrel (*F. dickinsoni*), 11 to 12 inches, is a lighter grey bird but with blackish wings and back. It is found from Tanzania to Mozambique and Angola where it occurs in low-lying country, often in small parties. It pursues locusts in the air and catches lizards and so on. It lays two or three eggs in the crown of a palm tree. The Barred Kestrel (*F. zoniventris*) of Madagascar, of which little is known, is 12 to 13 inches in size. It is also a grey bird, white below with brown bars.

The Red-footed Falcon (*F. vespertinus*), 11 to 12 inches, found from eastern Europe to eastern Asia in summer, migrates to Africa in winter. The male is grey with rufous thighs and vent. The female is rufous on the head and below, pale grey barred with dark grey above. Usually seen in flocks, these birds hawk insects high in the air. They breed colonially in old nests of the crow family and lay four or five eggs.

The Red-headed Merlin (*F. chiquera*), 11 to 13 inches, is found in open country in parts of southern Africa and in India. A fast, strongly-made bird, it catches birds up to the size of small doves and quail. It lays from two to four eggs in tree nests. The Merlin or Pigeon Hawk (*F. columbarius*), 10 to 13 inches, is found in northern Europe and Asia and in North America. A fast, usually low-level hunter generally in open country, it catches mainly small birds and in some areas large insects. It lays four or five eggs in an old nest on the ground, or in holes in trees or banks.

Red-headed Merlin

Hobbys

The Little Falcon (*F. longipennis*) of Australia, Timor, Flores and Ceram is 11 to 13 inches in size and is blue above, rufous on the hind neck, and duller below. A strong, dashing little bird, it hunts in open or lightly wooded country especially near water, where it catches birds as they fly in to drink. It nests high in a tree and lays three eggs. The Oriental Hobby (*F. severus*), 11 to 13 inches, occurs from the central Himalayas to the Solomon Islands. It is black above and on the head and reddish-chestnut below. It catches small birds, bats and insects over open wooded country, often hunting at dawn and dusk. It breeds in an old nest in a tree or on a rock ledge, usually laying two eggs. The African Hobby (*F. cuvieri*), 10 to 12 inches, is found in open and lightly wooded country in central, eastern and south-eastern Africa. It is greyish-black above, rufous below, and white on the cheeks and chin. It catches mainly large insects and some small birds, all taken on the wing. It breeds in an old nest in a tall tree. The European

Hobby (*F. subbuteo*), 12 to 14 inches, is found right across central Asia in summer, migrating to Africa and southern Asia in winter. It hawks high in the air for small birds, insects and bats. It is extremely fast, sometimes being able to catch swifts. It resembles a huge swift in shape when seen from below. It usually lays three or four eggs in an old crow's nest. The Bat Falcon (*F. rufigularis*), 9 to 12 inches, found from Mexico to northern Argentina, is a tiny but very strong, fast little hobby able to catch almost any small bird or large insect in the air. It can even catch the largest kinds of swifts if it can get above them, as it is perhaps the fastest of all small birds in a dive. It lays two or three eggs, usually in a cavity in trees.

Eleanora's Falcon (*F. eleanorae*), 14 to 15 inches, lives mostly on islands in the Mediterranean. It resembles a large long-tailed hobby but with no reddish colouring below. Some birds are blackish throughout. They feed mostly on birds up to the size of Hoopoes. Because birds are most plentiful at the time of the autumn migration, they breed at this time, laying two or three eggs on a cliff ledge. The Sooty Falcon (*F. concolor*) of eastern Africa and Madagascar is 12 to 13 inches in size and is a blackish-grey bird with dark brown wings found in open woodland as well as in desert and on islands. Like the last species, it preys on migrant birds. It also catches bats and insects. It lays three eggs among rocks. There is also a dark phase which occurs.

Hobby in flight and at rest

Gyr Falcon — Iceland race

Large Falcons

The Black Falcon (*F. subniger*), 17 to 19 inches, is a blackish-brown falcon generally found in open or lightly wooded country inland in Australia, where it preys on medium-sized birds. It lays three or four eggs in an old nest of another bird. The New Zealand Falcon (*F. novaezeelandiae*), 15 to 18 inches, is blackish-brown above, buffish-white with brown streaks below, and reddish on the thighs and undertail coverts. Its prey consists of small birds, rodents, lizards and insects. It usually lays three eggs on a rocky ledge. The Aplomado Falcon (*F. femoralis*), 13 to 17 inches, occurs from the southern United

Saker Falcon

States to Tierra del Fuego. It is grey above, white below with heavy black bars on the underparts, and buffy-orange on the thighs, undertail, and sometimes on the breast and collar. It catches large insects, small birds, rodents, small snakes and lizards. It builds a low tree nest in dry country.

The Grey Falcon (*F. hypoleucos*), 12 to 16 inches, inhabits the drier and mountainous regions of Australia. It preys mainly on small marsupials, reptiles and birds. The Laggar Falcon (*F. jugger*), of India is 15 to 17 inches in size and is ashy-brown above with a dull rufous crown, and whitish below with dark streaks from the lower breast downwards, with brown flanks and thighs. It is an agile flier and can take birds up to the size of partridges. The Lanner Falcon (*F. biarmicus*), 15 to 18 inches, is found in south-eastern Europe and most of the drier parts of Africa. It catches a large variety of birds and also kills rodents and lizards. It nests on a rock ledge or in an old nest in trees.

The Prairie Falcon (*F. mexicanus*), 16 to 19 inches, inhabits

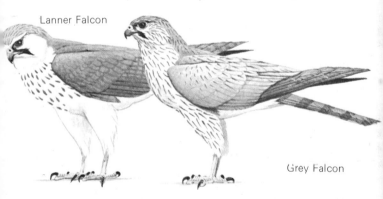

Lanner Falcon

Grey Falcon

dry open country in the western United States, south-western Canada and Mexico. It looks similar to the Saker or Lanner but is brown throughout above. It preys on birds and rodents. It usually lays five eggs in a hollow or in a large deserted nest on a cliff. The Saker Falcon (*F. cherrug*) of south- eastern Europe and central Asia, which is 18 to 23 inches in size, migrates to Africa and India in winter. It can kill large birds and has been seen to kill an Imperial Eagle. It lays three to five eggs in a tree nest or sometimes on a cliff ledge.

Peale's Peregrine Falcon

Gyr and Peregrines

The Gyr Falcon (*F. rusticolus*) of the Arctic regions is 20 to 23 inches in size and may be any colour from clear white with a few dark marks to almost completely black. Usually the lightest birds occur in the far north and darkest farther south. These are the largest, heaviest falcons and they have the broadest wings. They are very fast in level flight and pursue Ptarmigans, auks, waterfowl, waders and occasionally gulls and Arctic Hares. They feed largely on lemmings when these are abundant. They usually lay four eggs in a nest (often the old nest of a Raven) on a cliff ledge. Because of their speed these birds were, and still are, a favourite of falconers.

The Taita Falcon (*F. fasciinucha*), 11 to 13 inches, occurs in a few drier parts of eastern Africa. It resembles the African Hobby, but the chestnut underparts extend to the nape and it has the build of a tiny Peregrine. It catches pigeons and smaller birds after a low-level chase. Its nesting habits are unknown. The Orange-breasted Falcon (*F. deiroleucos*), 13 to 15 inches, is found from Mexico to Argentina. It is similar to the Taita but has a black area on the lower breast and has a dark nape. It is even more Peregrine-like in build, and

Barbary Falcon

Peregrine Falcon in flight

presumably hunts medium-sized birds. Little is recorded about this bird or Kleinschmidt's Falcon (*F. kreyenborgi*), which is 15 to 17 inches in size, and which is hobby-like in the shape of its wings and tail but resembles a pale Peregrine in colour and build (except the head which is buff like that of a Lanner). It inhabits southern Argentina and Chile, where it breeds on rock ledges. The Peregrine Falcon (*F. peregrinus*), 13 to 19 inches, is found almost throughout the world except in the high Arctic, high mountains and tropical forest areas. It is a heavily-built bird which enables it to dive at speeds of up to 200 miles an hour. Ducks, pigeons, waders, sea birds and small birds are the usual prey. Large birds are generally struck behind the head or upper wing with the hind claws as the falcon shoots by. Small birds are carried off. The plumage varies in different parts of the world; birds from the west coast of North America are very dark, tropical birds usually have black heads, and desert birds – known as Barbary Falcons – are small and pale. They lay two to four eggs on a cliff ledge, building, old nest in a tree, or occasionally, on the ground. They may also nest on high buildings in cities.

Barn and Bay Owls

The Barn Owl (*Tyto alba*), 11 to 16 inches, is found in temperate regions where winter temperatures are not very low, and most of the tropical parts of the world except in deserts and dense forests. The plumage is very variable. Barn Owls live almost entirely on rodents, so are beneficial to Man. Their eyes are rather small for a nocturnal bird, but their ears take up almost the whole length of the skull so the prey is located by sound. The call is an eerie shriek, and hissing, snoring, and chuckling notes are also uttered. The wings are long and the owl can glide silently over meadows or open woodland country. Its abundance depends on the number of rodents, and when these are plentiful Barn Owls have been known to lay twice in one year. There are normally four to six eggs, laid in buildings, hollow trees, holes in cliffs or old nests of other birds. The Grass Owl (*T. capensis*), 13 to 16 inches, found in southern Africa, parts of south-eastern Asia and Australia in open grassland, is generally darker above than is the Barn Owl. The tiny Madagascar Grass Owl (*T. soumagnei*), 10 inches, is very dark in colour. The large Celebes Barn Owl (*T. rosenbergii*), 15

Barn Owl — light-
and dark-breasted forms

to 19 inches, is equally dark. Just as large is the Masked Owl (*T. novaehollandiae*), of Tasmania. Females of this form are over twice the weight of males and are able to catch rabbits, rat-kangaroos and Ring-tailed Opossums. Individuals from the mainland of Australia are smaller. This species lays only two or three eggs. The Sooty Owl (*T. tenebricosa*), 12 to 14 inches, is spotted dark brown above and light below in Australia, and dark brown throughout in New Guinea. The New Britain Barn Owl (*T. aurantia*), 10 to 12 inches, and the Minahassa Barn Owl (*T. inexspectata*) of Celebes, which is 10 to 12 inches in size, are both brown with typical barn owl markings above.

The Bay Owl (*Phodilus badius*), 10 inches, lives in forests from central India to Borneo and Java. It spends its day in a hole in a tree. It is very sluggish, more so even than the Barn Owl, and lays two to four eggs. Food is less specialized than is the Barn Owl's, and it will eat rodents, small birds, lizards, frogs and beetles. The call notes resemble a mixture of those of barn, scops and wood owls. The Congo Bay Owl (*P. prigoginei*), a darker bird with smaller feet, was not discovered until 1951.

Masked Owl (female)

Bay Owl

White-faced Scops Owl

European Scops Owl

Scops Owls

The Scops Owl (*Otus scops*), $6\frac{1}{2}$ to 8 inches, is found over most of the tropical and warmer temperate parts of the Old World anywhere where cover is sufficient. At night their call betrays their presence. Food is almost entirely insects. They nest in holes. The Mountain Scops Owl (*O. spilocephalus*), 7 to 9 inches, occurs up to 7,000 feet from the Himalayas to Borneo. It is spotted above. The Andaman Scops Owl (*O. balli*), 8 inches, has a dark reddish back.

The Reddish Scops Owl (*O. rufescens*) of Malaya, Sumatra, Java and Borneo is orange-brown with paler eyebrows and forehead. In Celebes, the Sunda Islands and Moluccas, the Celebes Scops Owl (*O. manadensis*), $7\frac{1}{2}$ to 9 inches, occurs. The Flores Scops Owl (*O. alfredi*), $7\frac{1}{2}$ inches, is orange-brown with white markings. A similar owl, the Mentaur Scops Owl (*O. umbra*), $6\frac{1}{2}$ inches, lives in Engano and Simalur islands off Sumatra. The Palau Scops Owl (*O. podarginus*), $8\frac{1}{2}$ inches, and

Screech Owl — dark and light phases

the Wiak Scops Owl (*O. beccarii*) of the Schouten Islands off New Guinea, are both heavily barred. The Flammulated Owl (*O. flammeolus*) of the Rocky Mountains from British Columbia to southern Mexico is 6 inches in size. The Russet Scops Owl (*O. rutila*) of Madagascar, the Comoros and Pemba Islands is 7 to 9 inches in size, and chestnut-brown, or russet above and grey and brown below. In western Africa, the Cinnamon Scops Owl (*O. icterorhynchus*), 7 to 8 inches, is smaller. A smaller species (*O. ireneae*), greyer in colour, was discovered in eastern Africa as recently as 1965.

These next species take more rodents, small birds and lizards. The White-faced Scops Owl (*O. leucotis*) of Africa south of Gambia and the central Sudan is 8 to 10 inches in size. The White-fronted Scops Owl (*O. sagittatus*), 10 to 11½ inches, is found from southern Burma to Malaya. The Giant Scops Owl (*O. gurneyi*), 12 inches, is known only from Mindanao and Marinduque in the Philippines. The Collared Scops Owl (*O.*

bakkamoena), 7 to 9½ inches, from Muscat in Arabia to Japan and Java is similar to the Screech Owl but browner. The Seychelles Owl (*O. insularis*), thought extinct, has lately been heard calling. The Rajah Scops Owl (*O. brookei*) of Borneo, Sumatra and Java is 9 inches in size and like a Collared but has more white. The Lesser Sunda Scops Owl (*O. silvicola*), 10 inches, is similar to the Collared. The Screech Owl (*O. asio*), 7 to 9 inches, is common in the United States and parts of southern and western Canada. There is also an intermediate phase. The Whiskered Screech Owl (*O. trichopsis*), 7 inches, occurs from the Arizona Canyons to Honduras. The Pacific Screech Owl (*O. cooperi*), 8 inches, occurs in low, dry country from southern Mexico to Costa Rica. The Spix Screech Owl (*O. choliba*), 7 to 8 inches, from Costa Rica to northern Argentina, is finely barred below. The Puerto Rican Screech Owl (*O. nudipes*), 8 to 10 inches, is similar to the Screech Owl without ear tufts and has bare legs, as has the Cuban Bare-legged Owl (*O. lawrencii*), 8 inches. The Bearded

Crested Owl

Akun Eagle Owl

Screech Owl (*O. barbarus*) of southern Mexico and Guatemala, and the Dark-crowned Screech Owl (*O. roboratus*) of Ecuador and Peru have white collars. The Tawny-bellied Screech Owl (*O. watsonii*), 8 to 9 inches, found from Colombia to Argentina, is dark above and orange-rufous with dark marks below. The Brazilian Black-capped Screech Owl (*O. atricapillus*) is another dark species. The Vermiculated Screech Owl (*O. guatemalae*), 8 to 9 inches, found from Mexico to Bolivia, is very dark below. The Rufescent Screech Owl (*O. ingens*), 9 to 11 inches, is similar but has no ear tufts. It occurs from Colombia to Bolivia, as does the White-throated Screech Owl (*O. albogularis*), 11 inches. The Bare-shanked Screech Owl (*O. clarkii*) occurs in Panama and Costa Rica.

The Maned Owl (*Jubula lettii*), 11 inches, found from Sierra Leone to western Kenya, is rare, as is the Crested Owl (*Lophostrix cristata*), 17 inches, from southern Mexico to the Amazon.

The Akun Eagle Owl (*Bubo leucostictus*) of west African forests is mainly insectivorous. It has a chittering call.

Maned Owl

Eagle Owls

Fraser's Eagle Owl (*B. poensis*), 14 to 18 inches, occurs in western African forests. It has an orange-yellow face, is brown above and white finely barred with brown below. A subspecies in the Amani forest in Tanzania is heavily marked with brown below. The call of these birds is a long series of short, deep hoots. The Malay Eagle Owl (*B. sumatrana*), 16 to 18 inches, occurs from southern Burma to Borneo and Bali. It is rather like the Fraser's but has longer barred ear tufts. The Forest Eagle Owl (*B. nipalensis*), 20 to 24 inches, is found over most of India, Ceylon, and east to Vietnam. It is not unlike a large, heavily-marked Malay bird. It kills small mammals including flying squirrels, birds, snakes and lizards. The Dusky Eagle Owl (*B. coromandus*), 19 to 22 inches, lives in small woods and groves from India to Malaysia. It is greyish-brown mottled with white, and has deep yellow eyes. Its prey is mainly crows taken at their roosts at night.

The Milky Eagle Owl (*B. lacteus*) of Africa south of the Sahara is 21 to 23 inches in size and is very nocturnal, almost torpid by day. Shelley's Eagle Owl (*B. shelleyi*), 24 inches, the large eagle owl of West African forests, is dark-eyed, barred dark brown and white. The Spotted Eagle Owl (*B. africanus*), 13 to 17 inches, inhabits rocky country over most of Africa and southern Arabia. It is mottled white, grey and black throughout, with brown markings below. The Cape Eagle Owl (*B. capensis*), 19 to 21 inches, is found on high mountains in southern and eastern Africa and resembles the next species in habits and appearance. The Great Eagle Owl (*B. bubo*) of Europe, Asia and North Africa is 17 to 30 inches in size and is very variable. The bird illustrated is a small desert form from Arabia; the largest birds occur in Siberia and Turkestan. These can kill mammals, birds nearly their own size, reptiles and insects. The call of this and the two previous species is a low double hoot. The Great Horned Owl (*B. virginianus*), 18 to 23 inches, occurs from central Alaska and Labrador to the Straits of Magellan. Rabbits are its favourite food in many areas but it also attacks skunks, porcupines, birds, and snakes.

Great Horned Owl (*top*), Desert Eagle Owl (*centre*), Milky Eagle Owl (*bottom*)

Brown Fish Owl

Its main call is a series of five to seven low hoots. Eagle owls lay their one to three eggs on rock ledges or crevices, in old nests of other birds, or in depressions in the ground in flat, treeless country. The Philippine Eagle Owl (*B. philippensis*), 17 inches, is little known. Dark orange above, paler below and streaked dark brown throughout, it looks rather like a fish owl.

Fish Owls and Snowy Owl

Blakiston's Fish Owl (*Ketupa blakistoni*) of north-eastern Asia is 18 to 23 inches, pale-coloured with brown streaks and reddish-brown bars. It is feathered to the toes to prevent frost-bite. The Tawny Fish Owl (*K. flavipes*), 19 to 21 inches, occurs from the lower Himalayas to southern China and Vietnam. It is pale rufous-brown streaked with grey-brown. The lower legs are feathered half way down. In the next two species the lower legs are completely bare. The Malay Fish

Pel's Fishing Owl

Owl (*K. ketupa*), 17 to 18 inches, found from Burma to Borneo, is pale amber-brown with darker brown streaks. The Brown Fish Owl (*K. zeylonensis*), 19 to 21 inches, occurs from southern Turkey to southern China. These owls are found in trees near fresh water up to 7,000 feet and in addition to fish eat small mammals, birds, reptiles, crabs and insects. They normally lay two eggs in a hole.

Pel's Fishing Owl (*Scotopelia peli*), 21 to 24 inches, is from Africa below the Sahara. The Rufous Fishing Owl (*S. ussheri*) is more variable in colour but less heavily barred. It is confined to western African rain forests, as is Bouvier's Fishing Owl (*S. bouvieri*), 15 to 17 inches, which is darker above and white heavily streaked below. The food of these species appears to be almost entirely fish. They lay four eggs.

The Snowy Owl (*Nyctea scandiaca*), 21 to 24 inches, lives in barren Arctic regions but flies south in winter where it

male

female

Snowy Owl

occurs on moors and coastal marshes. Although it can kill prey up to the size of geese and hares, its main food in the Arctic is the lemming. When these are scarce it may not attempt to breed, but when they are plentiful up to ten eggs may be laid in a depression on a rise in the ground.

Pygmy Owls and Elf Owl

The pygmy owls hunt small mammals, birds, lizards, snakes and large insects. They are strong for their size and able to kill prey larger than themselves. They hunt during morning and evening in either dark or daylight. The calls are often musical. They lay three to five eggs in holes in trees. The Eurasian Pygmy Owl (*Glaucidium passerinum*), $6\frac{1}{2}$ inches, lives in coniferous forests in mountain areas. The Collared Owlet (*G. brodiei*), 6 to $6\frac{1}{2}$ inches, has a brown and red phase and comes from south-eastern Asia. The Jungle Owlet (*G. radi-*

atum), $6\frac{1}{2}$ to 7 inches, of India also has two phases. The Large Barred Owlet (*G. cuculoides*), 8 to 10 inches, occurs in the Himalayas, China and Java. Four species occur in Africa: the Pearl-spotted Owlet (*G. perlatum*), $6\frac{1}{2}$ inches, is found over most of Africa south of the Sahara. The Red-chested Owlet (*G. tephronotum*), $6\frac{1}{2}$ inches, lives in parts of western and central Africa. The Barred Owlet (*G. capense*), 8 inches, occurs in southern Africa and the largest of all, the Chestnut-backed Owlet (*G. sjostedti*), 10 inches, comes from the Cameroon. The Americas have five species: the Northern Pygmy Owl (*G. gnoma*), 6 inches, occurs in the region of the Rocky Mountains. The Andean Pygmy Owl (*G. jardinii*), 5 to $5\frac{1}{2}$ inches, replaces it as far as Peru. The Brazilian Pygmy Owl (*G. brazilianum*), $6\frac{1}{2}$ inches, occurs from Arizona to southern South America. There is also the Cuban Pygmy Owl (*G. siju*), $6\frac{1}{2}$ inches, and the tiny Least Pygmy Owl (*G. minutissimum*), $5\frac{1}{2}$ to 6 inches, found from Mexico to Brazil.

The smallest owl, the Elf Owl (*Micrathene whitneyi*), $5\frac{1}{4}$ inches, lives in the deserts of the south-western United States and Mexico. Almost entirely insectivorous, it hunts only at night. It roosts by day and lays its eggs – usually three in number – in woodpeckers' holes bored in the giant cactus.

Eurasian Pygmy Owl

Elf Owl

Little Owl

Little Owls

The Little Owl (*Athene noctua*), 7 to 9 inches, is found over most of Europe, western and central Asia, parts of northern Africa and New Zealand, where it has been introduced. It is generally fairly common in agricultural countryside, hunting mostly at dawn and dusk. Its flight is undulating like the woodpecker's. The calls are variable but two rather plaintive similar notes are most often heard. It lays two to five eggs. The Spotted Owlet (*A. brama*), common from western India to Laos, is similar but lives almost entirely on insects. The rare, little-known Forest Spotted Owlet (*A. blewitti*), 9 inches, occurs in forest areas in central and eastern India.

The Burrowing Owl (*Speotyto cunicularia*), 7 to 9 inches, occurs from south-western Canada to southern South America, in Florida and some of the Caribbean Islands. It lives in uncultivated flat country and prairies. It spends the day in holes in the ground, emerging in the evening to hunt.

Tengmalm's or Boreal Owl (*Aegolius funereus*), 10 inches, lives in coniferous woods in northern and eastern Europe, central Asia, Alaska and parts of Canada. It normally hunts at night for rodents, small birds, frogs and insects. The call resembles the sound of water dripping. There are usually

Tengmalm's Owl

Burrowing Owl

three to six eggs laid in a hole in a tree. The Saw-whet Owl (*A. acadicus*), $6\frac{1}{2}$ to $7\frac{1}{2}$ inches, occurs from south-eastern Alaska and central Labrador to Mexico, but not in the south-eastern United States. It is browner than Tengmalm's. Completely nocturnal, it hunts mostly mice. The Unspotted Saw-whet Owl (*A. ridgwayi*), 7 inches, found from southern Mexico to Costa Rica, is similar, but lacks spots and bars on the wings and tail. The Buff-fronted Owl (*A. harrisii*), 7 to $8\frac{1}{2}$ inches, occurs in Venezuela, Colombia and Ecuador, and in south-eastern Brazil and northern Argentina. It is dark brown above.

119

Brown Hawk Owl   New Guinea Hawk Owl

Hawk Owls

The Hawk Owl (*Surnia ulula*), 14 to 15 inches, inhabits northern conifer and birch forests in the Old and New Worlds. It hunts by daylight. When hungry it can kill birds its own size. It breeds in holes, in trees or in old nests.

Little is known about the New Guinea Hawk Owl (*Uroglaux dimorpha*), 10 to 11 inches, which has a long tail and very fine barring below.

The Brown Hawk Owl (*Ninox scutulata*), 9 to 12 inches, is found from Ceylon to eastern Siberia and Borneo. It hawks large insects in flight and will also take mice, small birds and shore crabs. A smaller bird, the Andaman Hawk Owl (*N. affinis*), 9 inches, occurs in those islands, together with the Brown Hawk Owl. The Philippine Hawk Owl (*N. philippensis*), 6 to 8 inches, varies in appearance. Only one species has reached the West, the Madagascar Hawk Owl (*N. superciliaris*), 9 to 11 inches. Celebes has two species – the Speckled Hawk Owl (*N. punctulata*) and the Ochre-bellied Hawk Owl (*N.*

perversa), both 8 to 10 inches long. The Moluccan Hawk Owl (*N. squampilia*), 10 to 14 inches, varies considerably in colour. The Sooty-backed Hawk Owl (*N. theomacha*), 8 to 10 inches, is the small owl of lowland forests in New Guinea. The New Britain Hawk Owl (*N. odiosa*) is spotted white above like the last species. The New Ireland Hawk Owl (*N. solomonis*), 9 to 11 inches, is also in New Britain. The Solomon Islands Hawk Owl (*N. jacquinoti*), 8 to 10 inches, varies considerably. Also in this area is the Admiralty Islands Hawk Owl (*N. meeki*), 9 to 12 inches. The Winking Owl (*N. connivens*), 10 to 18 inches, occurs on Halmerhera, eastern New Guinea and in Australia except for the interior. Australian birds are the largest. The Boobook Owl (*N. novaeseelandiae*), 10 to 14 inches, occurs from the south Moluccas to New Zealand and is very variable. The Rufous Owl (*N. rufa*), 17 to 18 inches, lives in lowland forests in New Guinea and northern Australia. The Powerful Owl (*N. strenua*), 20 to 23 inches, of south-eastern Australia, is capable of killing rabbits and opossums.

Powerful Owl

Spectacled Owl

Laughing and Tropical Wood Owls

The Laughing Owl (*Scelo-glaux albifacies*), 13 to 15 inches, which once lived in most parts of New Zealand, is now confined to a few places in South Island. It feeds on rodents, lizards, worms, and insects, and lays its three eggs in holes in cliffs.

The Spectacled Owl (*Pul-satrix perspicillata*), 16 to 19 inches, is found from southern Mexico to Argentina. It lives in heavy tropical forest, preying on small mammals and insects, and lays two eggs

African Wood Owl

Laughing Owl

in a hole in a tree. Its call sounds like a woodpecker tapping. The Rusty Barred Owl (*P. melanota*), 19 inches, is similar but has white eyebrows and is white below with brown bars. It occurs in Ecuador and Peru. In southern Brazil, the White-chinned Owl (*P. koeniswaldiana*), 17 inches, has yellow-orange on the eyebrows and below, and a white barred tail.

The African Wood Owl (*Ciccaba woodfordii*), 11 to 13 inches, found over most of Africa south of the Sahara, frequents forest edges, woods and dense bush along the banks of streams. It hunts by night when its loud three-syllabled call with the accent on the last note is frequently heard. One egg is the usual clutch. The Mottled Owl (*C. virgata*), 12 to 14 inches, occurs in mountain and tropical forests from Mexico to Argentina. It is dark brown with light spots above, white or tawny heavily streaked with deep brown below. The Black and White Owl (*C. nigrolineata*), 13 to 15 inches, found from southern Mexico to western Ecuador, is white barred with black below extending to the upper back, and black elsewhere above. The Black-Banded Owl (*C. huhula*), 16 inches, is an Amazonian forest species which is black throughout, barred with white.

Great Grey Owl

Wood Owls

The Rufous-banded Owl (*C. albitarsus*), 16 inches, occurs in the Andean forests from Venezuela to Ecuador.

The Great Grey Owl (*Strix nebulosa*), 27 inches, occurs in coniferous forests from Scandinavia, across central Siberia to parts of northern and western North America. It appears to be much larger than it really is owing to the volume of its feathers, which are insulation from the cold conditions under which it lives. It preys on squirrels, rats, mice and occasionally birds. The Barred Owl (*S. varia*), 17 to 19 inches, occurs from southern Canada to Honduras. It nests in an old nest or in a tree cavity. The Spotted Owl (*S. occidentalis*), 16 to 18 inches, of western North America, is similar but is barred throughout below, more spotted above. Two South American wood owls are the Rufous-legged Owl (*S. rufipes*) from the south and the Brazilian Owl (*S. hylophila*). The Tawny Owl (*S. aluco*), 13 to 16 inches, is common in wooded areas in Europe, across Asia to China, and in north-western Africa. It preys mainly on mice, but rats or small rabbits may be taken. Where rodents are

Striped Owl

Barred Owl

scarce, birds form the main prey. Worms are eaten in wet weather, and frogs and insects occasionally. It lays two to four eggs in a hole in a tree or in an old nest of large birds. Hume's Tawny Owl (*S. butleri*), 12 inches, known only from coastal Baluchistan, Palestine and Sinai, is more buff in colour. The Ural Owl (*S. uralensis*), of eastern Europe and central Asia, 24 inches in size, is buff, heavily streaked below. South east Asia has three species: The Mottled Wood Owl (*S. ocellata*), 16 to 18 inches, of India and Arakan, the Brown Wood Owl (*S. leptogrammica*), 13 to 20 inches, from India and Ceylon to Formosa and Java, and the Pagoda Owl (*S. seloputo*), 16 to 18 inches, from south Burma to Java.

The little-known Striped Owl (*Rhinoptynx clamator*), 13 to 15 inches, occurs from southern Mexico to north Argentina.

Long-eared Owl

Short-eared Owl

Eared Owls

The Long-eared Owl (*Asio otus*), 13 to 14 inches, occurs in most of Europe, central Asia, southern Canada and most of the United States. A woodland bird although with rather long wings, it lives on small mammals, birds up to the size of Jays, and insects. It lays four or five eggs in an old squirrel's drey, in old nests, or on the ground. Its usual call is a low cooing moan uttered about every three seconds. The Long-eared Owl is decidedly a nocturnal and arboreal species and consequently is not often seen. The Abyssinian Long-eared Owl (*A. abyssinicus*), 14 to 16 inches, is darker and heavier marked above than is the Long-eared. It occurs on Mount Kenya, the Ruwenzori range, and the highlands of Ethiopia which was once called Abyssinia. The Madagascar Long-eared Owl (*A. madagascariensis*), 13 inches, is similar to the others but has orange-yellow in the plumage. The Stygian Owl (*A. stygius*) is found in forests – and often in mountains – from Mexico to northern Argentina. It also has prominent ear tufts. It is sooty above marked with orange, buff, white, and blotched and barred blackish below. The Short-eared Owl (*A. flammeus*), 14 to 16 inches, is found over most of the southern Arctic and temperate regions of the world. It hunts open country by day as well as by night and can often be identified in flight by the large, yellowish patch on each wing. It is a long-winged bird which glides low to surprise rodents or sometimes small birds on the ground. It makes a hollow in vegetation on the ground for its eggs – – usually four to eight, but it lays up to fourteen in a rodent plague. The African Marsh Owl (*A. capensis*), 12 to 15 inches, is another short-horned species, browner than the Short-eared. It has rather similar habits but lives mainly on large insects.

The Jamaican Owl (*Pseudoscops grammicus*), 11 to 13 inches, inhabits Jamaican woodlands. The normal clutch is two eggs laid in a cavity in a tree. Little else is known about it.

The Fearful Owl (*Nesasio solomonensis*), 15 inches, lives in forests on Bougainville, Choiseul and Ysabel in the Solomon Islands. The feet and bill are exceptionally powerful for an owl of its size and it is thought to kill opossums and medium-sized birds. It is, however, one of the rarer species of owl.

Jamaican Owl

Fearful Owl

LIFE AND HABITS

Life and Death

Most birds of prey – in common with most other birds – never see their first birthday. In many species it is estimated that three-quarters of the young which hatch die during their first year. Failure to find a suitable unoccupied territory and inexperience are the main causes. In some parts of the world many get shot, including unfortunately those which are of great benefit to agriculture, because at an early age their awareness of danger is relatively undeveloped.

Their inexperience at hunting causes young birds to attack unsuitable quarry and they often become tired after a long fruitless chase and collide with a tree or a rock. Most birds of prey found injured are first-year birds, and an injured immature has little chance of survival since it has no mate to hunt for it. Young birds also often choose unsuitable places for roosting and may be killed by other predators during the night. They may be attacked by large owls if they are small species,

Broken and worn claws   Bumble foot

and mammals such as Leopards and Wolverines have been known to kill the larger species while they are roosting. They may also be weakened or killed by the weather in countries which have low temperatures or hurricane-force winds.

Once a bird of prey has survived a year it will have developed a knowledge of what to do to survive and of what not to do. Large eagles which lay only one egg in their clutch are known to live for an average of fifteen years.

Disease is not a common cause of death, but the feet are vulnerable to injury. As killing weapons, great strain is frequently put upon them and small cuts or splits may allow infection to enter and cause swellings which render the feet useless. The kidneys of birds also seem vulnerable to infection and injury. Respiratory diseases, especially pneumonia, will develop in birds which are in poor condition or very old. A further trouble which may eventually lead to death is broken or twisted claws, which limit killing ability. Beaks also become overgrown or deformed.

Fights to the death between two birds over territory or

Some beak deformities

mates are rare in all but a few species. All these birds are very well armed and the combatants would probably kill or seriously injure each other; so their strong talons are generally a deterrent to war.

A new source of danger to birds of prey and owls has arisen in recent years – insecticides. These chemicals are used on seeds, growing crops and trees and become absorbed by small animals and birds which eat the plants. If a predatory bird (or mammal) eats many of the smaller plant-eaters, it takes in the poison which they have eaten and this may cause infertility or death to the predator. This is one of the chief causes of the rapid decline of such magnificent birds as the Peregrine Falcon in Europe and Bald Eagle in America, and has also contributed to the reduction in numbers of the Sparrow Hawk in Great Britain.

Very large birds which lay one egg at a time and do not breed every year, such as condors and some of the large vultures, may have a potential life span of forty to sixty years. Some of the larger eagle owls may also live as long. Most of the larger eagles may live from thirty to forty years, and the larger carrion hawks have a similar life span. Bateleurs seem to be exceptionally long-lived eagles; two in captivity have lived to forty-five and fifty-five years. Small eagles, large hawks, buzzards and falcons, as well as the medium-sized owls, seem to have potential maximum life-spans of twenty to thirty years, although very occasionally one may exceed this. For the small hawks and falcons, fifteen years seems to be the maximum, but quite a few small owls seem to live for about twenty years.

Most of these figures are of course from birds kept in captivity. When they die, post mortems reveal their bodies to be in a similar condition to those of humans aged between seventy and ninety.

The chart opposite shows some of the maximum ages recorded for captive birds:

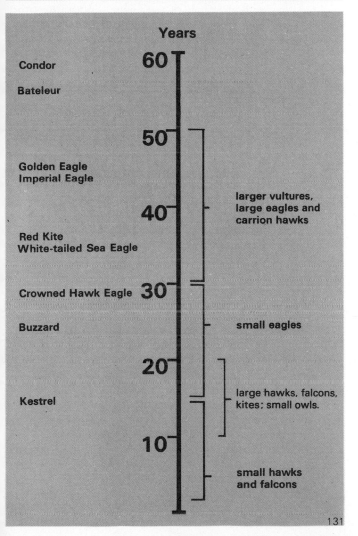

Longevity Chart
Maximum age recorded

Years

60

Condor

Bateleur

50

Golden Eagle
Imperial Eagle

40

larger vultures,
large eagles and
carrion hawks

Red Kite
White-tailed Sea Eagle

Crowned Hawk Eagle   30

Buzzard

small eagles

20

large hawks, falcons,
kites; small owls.

Kestrel

10

small hawks
and falcons

Territory

Many species of birds of prey are gregarious, especially those which live on carrion, fish, and insects. They often live in scattered colonies and in some cases may be seen hunting in groups, particularly those which catch insects in mid-air. The majority, however, as well as nearly all the owls, live in pairs on a territory or home range of their own. An ideal territory has certain basic characteristics. It contains sufficient available food for the whole year, with enough at one period to raise a brood of young. It has a choice of good nesting sites, and places to roost away from the wind in severe weather (in colder climates) and to give safety from human and other predators.

It follows that territories vary in size. A pair of small owls living in an area with a heavy mouse population may require as little as fifty acres. A Verreaux's Eagle – which specializes in catching Rock Hyraxes which live in colonies on isolated rocky hills in southern and eastern Africa – may have a territory of up to 250 square miles. It will need to hunt over several such hills, which may be scattered over a wide area, to provide food for both itself and its mate, and also for a young bird in some years.

Large forest eagles require almost as much room. Nests are seldom less than ten miles apart for such species as the Harpy and the Crowned Eagles. Certain species, harriers and Short-eared Owls for example, defend a territory during the breeding season but may, at other times of the year, congregate in a communal roost from which they fly off in different directions to hunt for food.

The territories of most birds of prey vary between one and ten square miles. The range of prey taken is also important. For example, the Great Horned Owl, which takes a wide range of mammals and birds, may require only between one and two square miles in areas where prey is plentiful.

In some parts of western Scotland, the Golden Eagle may need to resort mainly to sheep and deer carrion for food during the winter months. Even on a territory of perhaps more than 100 square miles of snow-covered hillside, prey is very scarce and difficult to locate. Weather conditions may also make flying difficult for long periods.

Although territories may be large, nests may sometimes be

Verreaux's Eagle in typical territory

quite near to each other. A wood surrounded by open country or a wooded valley in open hill country may hold more than one nest, perhaps only a few hundred yards apart. The birds range away from their nests in different directions. Often not all parts of a territory are defended. Sometimes an area between territories which holds very little prey or is subject to disturbance may be visited occasionally by any of the neighbouring pairs of birds, some of which may attempt to hold a part of the area for themselves.

The area around the nest is that which is most strongly defended, although when birds have eggs or young they may become less active so as not to reveal the site of the nest to other birds or predators. The nesting area will be defended against any large bird which may be a threat to it, such as other birds of prey, owls, crows, or Ravens.

Those species which migrate obviously give up their claims to the territories and hunting areas which they have held during the breeding season. Many of them take over a kind of territory in their new wintering areas which is intended only as a source of food and is generally not so jealously defended.

In those birds of prey which do not migrate from their breeding areas in autumn, there are a number of things which may happen after the young have successfully left the nest and are able to fly. Sometimes the parent pair will stay in the same place or territory, although they do not defend it so strongly as they have done while breeding. Other birds wander over a very much larger area which may well include the recently held territories of other pairs of their own species. They may even in such cases live semi-gregariously with these pairs.

Often birds of prey will defend their territory after breeding against members of their own species, and also against other species which hunt in a similar manner to themselves or take the same prey and are, therefore, competition to them.

Owls generally defend their territory throughout the year and can be very aggressive towards intruders even outside the breeding season, especially when food is not plentiful.

Saw-whet Owl roosting in top of young fir tree. The territory of small owls often includes gardens.

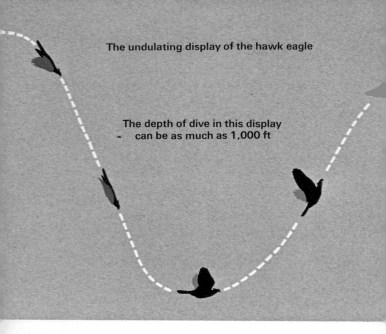

The undulating display of the hawk eagle

The depth of dive in this display can be as much as 1,000 ft

Displays

On sighting another bird of its own species or a species which may be a danger to its eggs or young, one or both of the territory owners sets off towards it in direct powerful flight. The meaning of this 'threat flight' is at once clear to the intruding bird, which normally turns and flies back. If it is merely trying to cross the range of its neighbours, it tries to avoid them by changing direction and going at full speed. If it is caught, a running fight may ensue. The intruder tries to avoid the blows of its pursuers. It probably gets buffeted but is unlikely to sustain real injury as neither side wants a really serious encounter. On reaching the boundary of their range, the aggressive owners usually turn for home or soar up in circles so that they can make sure that the intruder does not immediately return.

Other birds such as crows and Ravens and other raptors with overlapping ranges will be attacked if they enter the nesting area. But these birds will themselves attack should the bird of prey or owl venture into their nesting areas. Small

-birds of prey try to get behind and above a large one which is crossing their nesting area. By darting at it and screaming at it, they try to move it on. The intruder generally accelerates to escape their attentions and in so doing soon leaves the nesting area; their demonstration will have achieved its purpose.

In good weather, birds of prey frequently soar over and along the edge of their territory. This action marks out to other birds of the same species the area which the territory owners regard as their own.

Some of the forest eagles are not adept at soaring for very long periods owing to their short wings. So these birds have evolved spectacular displays – circling to a good height, diving to pick up speed, and then at the bottom of the dive suddenly shooting upwards using the momentum gained. The process is repeated several times, the bird crossing its territory in a series of undulations and emitting a loud piping call which can be heard for miles. Any nearby eagle can hear that this stretch of forest has been claimed.

This type of spectacular display is also performed to impress the bird's mate. A bird of prey dives at a tremendous speed, just missing its mate which may be perched or flying slowly. Or it may perform certain flight movements, such as cork-screws and loops, which look spectacular to human observers and probably also to other birds. A pair of Bald Eagles may join feet together while high in the air and then fall together, twisting over and over cart-wheel fashion.

Bald Eagles spiralling with claws interlocked

Owls whose courtship takes place in the Arctic summer or in early evening often give aerobatic displays. But to most owls these would be pointless as birds high in the air at night are almost invisible. The call notes figure largely in owls' displays, as well as bowing, wing clapping, mutual preening and bill touching, and courtship feeding (normally it is the male that brings food to his mate). This behaviour is also an important part of courtship in many of the birds of prey, especially

Threat display of Spotted Eagle Owl

among the smaller falcons. Mutual preening is also common among paired birds of prey. Female birds may beg food from the male rather in the manner of a young bird begging from its parent, and they also make chick-like noises.

Many owls puff out their feathers to impress their partner during courtship. This is also used to show aggression as it makes the bird appear much larger than it really is. Bill snapping is used, and the wings are opened and held forward. The owl may shuffle from one foot to the other, giving the impression of ferocity and that it is about to attack.

Many of the forest birds of prey possess a crest, which is raised and expanded to show aggression. The wings, if opened, are usually held with the undersides towards the intruder and the bird may lean back on its tail, making it possible to lash out with both feet in the event of an attack. Often a lot of noise is uttered at this time to inform the mate that an aggressor is present. Birds of prey and owls brooding eggs or young, however, if they see a large intruder, crouch low and keep completely still unless approached within a yard or two. Young chicks do not develop this habit until quite late so often give the nest site away by calling or moving.

Migration

Most of the birds of prey and owls which summer in areas that become very cold during the winter migrate to a warmer climate, as do most other birds. The main reason for this is the shortage of food. Many of the northern mammals hibernate for the winter and others live mostly under the snow; most of the small birds have gone. Reptiles, amphibians and insects are hidden away and most fish are under the ice. Certain tropical birds of prey also migrate from one area to another, especially in areas affected by periods of rain or drought.

In Europe most of the birds of prey leave Scandinavia. Falsterbo, near the southern tip of Sweden, is a place where various migration routes meet. Thousands of Common and Rough-legged Buzzards, Honey Buzzards, large numbers of Kestrels and Sparrow Hawks, and various eagles, Goshawks, and Ospreys may be seen on a single day if the weather is suitable for migration (dry and sunny with a fresh breeze).

Many of the eastern European birds of prey leave via the Bosphorus. Imperial, Steppe, Lesser and Greater Spotted Eagles may all be seen together there, as well as Short-toed, Booted and White-tailed, as they cross the narrow sea. Peregrines, Sakers, Lanners, Lesser Kestrels and Red-footed Falcons and many others go with them. With the exception of harriers and one or two falcons, birds of prey find travelling across wide stretches of water difficult as the warm air currents on which they depend to gain height are absent. It is not surprising therefore to find the Strait of Gibraltar the place where most of the western European migrants cross into Africa – although some of the birds of prey which migrate through passes in the Pyrenees go no farther south than Spain.

Apart from Gyr Falcons and Golden Eagles, most birds of prey leave northern Asia for India, south-eastern Asia and the Malay Archipelago. Many migrants, Hobbys and Peregrines, Steppe Eagles, and so on, cross the Himalayas in the autumn and return in spring. Two small hawks of eastern Asia – the Chinese Goshawk and the Rufous-winged Buzzard – migrate south-east in winter, some reaching as far as New Guinea. But the longest migration in the Old World is made by the Eastern Red-footed Falcon which breeds in north-eastern China and winters in Rhodesia. They fly via eastern India but

Autumn migration in Old World

observation points
general drift
broad front migration
concentrated migration
Red-footed Falcon (eastern race)

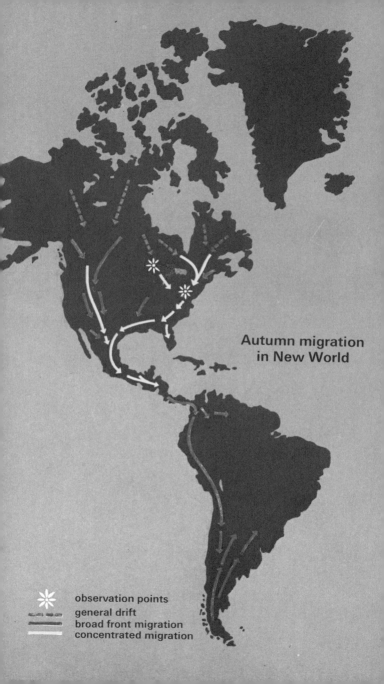

Autumn migration
in New World

we do not know for certain whether they then fly across the Indian Ocean, although they have not been seen anywhere between India and Kenya. They are known to be extremely fat before their departure, a condition common to many birds which migrate across large areas where food is unobtainable.

Northern owls are less adapted to migration than are the northern birds of prey. Both Long-eared and Short-eared Owls – long-winged species – migrate considerable distances. But most are not equipped for sustained flight so have to endure the long cold winter, although most move to sheltered woodlands in the valleys. Their plumage is extremely thick – three-quarters of what one sees when looking at a Great Grey Owl is feathers – and their feet are well feathered. Also their habit of roosting in holes helps keep them warm. But even so food is hard to find and many perish in hard weather.

Snowy Owls and most birds of prey tend to move south in hard winters in North America, often in considerable numbers. In the east, the Appalachian range forms one of the main routes and, at places such as Hawk Mountain in Pennsylvania, up to 20,000 birds may be seen during a year. Broad-winged and Red-tailed Buzzards and Sharp-shinned Hawks are the commonest species, but Turkey Vultures, Ospreys, Cooper's, Goshawks, Peregrines, Merlins and several others may be seen.

The Great Lakes form a barrier to hawk migration and thousands of birds of prey fly round the western end of Lake Superior and south along the shores of Lake Michigan. The little Broad-winged Hawk of eastern North America migrates as far as western Brazil and Peru – some 4,000 miles. However one of the species which migrates in the region of the Rocky mountains – Swainson's Buzzard – makes a round trip of up to 17,000 miles every winter as most of them fly as far as the pampas of northern Argentina. Some species breeding in southern Argentina, such as the Aplomado Falcon and the Cinereous Harrier, migrate northwards in the southern winter. Some of the insectivorous species such as the Swallow-tailed and Plumbeous Kites breeding in the north of the country move farther northwards into Brazil in the cooler weather, just as their opposite numbers in the southern United States and Mexico move southwards into central America during the northern winter.

KEEPING BIRDS OF PREY

Falconry

The art of falconry has been carried on in Asia for more than 4,000 years and has flourished there in various forms since that time. Today, it is widely practised in Arabia, Turkestan, parts of India and Pakistan, and to a limited extent in Japan. In central Asia, Golden Eagles are used to kill wolves and foxes and the Bonelli's Eagle is used to catch gazelles. Arabs use the Saker to catch gazelles. This falcon is not strong enough to kill the quarry, but slows down the gazelle by hanging on until it can be reached by hounds which are trained to work with the birds. Arabs also use Peregrines and Lanners to catch bustards and other birds.

The Laggar replaces the Lanner in India and, although it is

Golden Eagle flying at Wolf

144

used against crows and partridges, the larger and stronger Peregrines and Sakers are preferred. The little Red-headed Merlin is used sometimes, against smaller birds. The Goshawk, although difficult to obtain in India, is very popular and Sparrow Hawks and Shikras are flown at small birds.

Falconry spread into Europe by 500 AD, and by the Middle Ages had become the sport for all who could afford it. After 1000 AD, most European kings spent vast sums on falconry establishments. First-class birds were sold for up to £1,000.

Falconry is practised quite extensively, although in a limited way, in northern Europe today. The birds are similar to those used in Asia, although recently several species from other parts of the world have been tried. Since early this century, falconry has gained a hold in the United States where some new species including the Cooper's Hawk have proved

Peregrine stooping at grouse

Goshawk on bow perch

themselves to be quite adaptable to this interesting sport.

Today, quite a few people in western countries want to become falconers but probably not more than one in fifty ever becomes competent at the sport. Western civilization does not produce people with the necessary qualifications; most people are forced to live in towns and they tend to be impatient in so many ways and seem to have no wish to spend time trying to understand things as they really are.

Even anyone with a deep ambition dedicated to practise falconry still finds it difficult to learn. Ideally he should try to learn from an expert – an expert being someone who believes he knows rather little about his craft but whom other people respect, whose birds live for a long time, appear in good condition and actually catch things. Such people are few.

Much can be learned from books on falconry but they are not enough; they cannot tell the learner what he is doing wrong.

A falconer must choose a bird which is suitable for hunting within the type of land he has at his disposal for the type of quarry which is available there. Normally short-winged hawks are used in fairly wooded country because this is where they hunt naturally. They do not fly far, so they do not get lost easily as would a falcon, which should be chosen only for very open country.

Young hawks are generally more easily trained than are adults, but the mature birds are usually better at hunting. When a falconer receives a bird, he often places a hood on its head to keep it quiet, and attaches a leather strap known as a *jess* to each leg. The jesses are fastened to one end of a steel swivel, the other end of which is attached to a leash by which the bird is tied to its perch (or sometimes, if it is a falcon, to its wooden or stone block). The perch or block is kept in a darkened quiet room or shed and – especially if the hawk is hooded – the bird gets the

Gyr Falcon on block

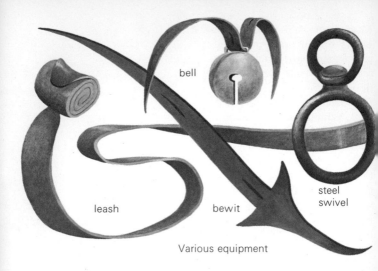

bell

leash

bewit

steel
swivel

Various equipment

impression that it is night and tends to calm down and relax.

A falconer carries the bird on his gloved fist up and down the room for long periods to get it used to being handled, often touching it with a small stick – which it will resent for some time but will eventually become used to. A morsel of food may be used instead of the stick, which the bird may snap at in anger and probably swallow if hungry. Small pieces of food may at first be flicked away in anger but eventually hunger should overcome this. After a while the bird begins to accept the food and then comes to expect small morsels which it devours readily. Large pieces can then be given and, finding these too large to swallow, it will then transfer them to its feet and begin to feed normally.

After this stage the light in the room may be increased gradually. Or, if the hawk is hooded, the hood may be removed for a few moments just as it is beginning to eat a particularly succulent piece of meat and when it is known to be hungry. If this is arranged and carried out carefully, the bird may continue feeding and not become upset. At first the falconer must turn his face away and never appear to stare directly at the bird or it will probably take fright.

When the hawk will remain steady on the falconer's glove in full light, the next step is to take the bird outside. Late on a

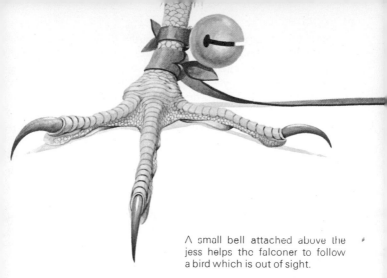

A small bell attached above the jess helps the falconer to follow a bird which is out of sight.

quiet, still evening is usually the best time. Then gradually the bird is made used to being carried about at other times of the day and is introduced to other people, animals, vehicles, and so on – first at a distance, gradually at closer ranges. At this stage the hawk is encouraged to jump from its perch to the fist for its food, if possible over a longer distance each day. It is then taken outside to a familiar place and encouraged to fly long distances to food while attached to a line called a *creance*.

When the falconer is certain the bird will fly directly to the fist automatically (a difficult thing to decide), he releases it from the creance when he knows it is hungry, and, having made certain that they will not be disturbed, he may safely fly the bird free for the first time. Before this time a hawk may be encouraged to take its food from a *lure*, which is a sort of dummy often made from leather and the wings of the bird the hawk is intended to fly at.

At first the lure (with a large piece of good meat tied to it) is simply tossed a foot or two in front of the sitting bird which will jump onto it if hungry. As it becomes accustomed to being fed from the lure, the falconer drags the lure along and the bird flies after it. Eventually the stage is reached when the bird will snatch at it as it is swung in the air. Falcons especially become very expert at this and are often exercised for long periods, the falconer jerking the lure away at the last moment so that the bird is forced to circle up and dive again. Falcons do not become annoyed; they seem to regard it as a game and know that they will be allowed to catch the lure eventually. The lure is the best way to encourage a bird to return if it seems disinclined to do so. A whistle is often used as the lure is swung to attract the bird's attention and the sight of the food moving below lures it down. An important aid to finding a bird which is lost or temporarily out of sight is a bell. The falconer generally attaches a small light bell to the hawk's leg just above the jess by a piece of leather known as a *bewit*.

Sometimes a bird of prey will decide to chase something else while waiting for the lure and may make its first kill this way. In many parts of the world, captive birds or animals may be released close to the hawk to encourage it to make its first kill. This method is, however, illegal in Britain today. Generally a falconer will try to get his bird close to its quarry, trying to choose one that is immature, in moult, or well away from cover to give his inexperienced bird a good chance. But some hawks become very tame and simply wait for food to be produced. Such birds, of no use to a falconer, may make good pets.

Experts do not recommend birds of prey or owls as pets for the average person. But to someone who has a deep interest in these birds and does not have the wish to practise falconry, they make interesting companions for a long time – for perhaps

Box cage diagram

Height slightly
greater than depth.

|← approx. 2 ft. →|

|← 3 – 4 ft →|

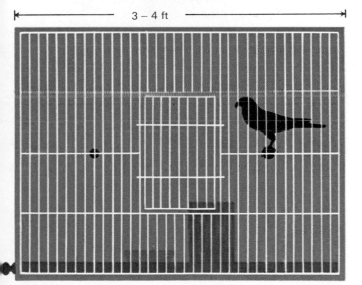

Shed for larger birds

all of a person's life. Whereas relatively few species of birds of prey are suitable for falconry, most species may make good pets, as do most kinds of owls.

The choice of species depends partly on the accommodation available (on whether the owner has a flat in town or a large garden in the country). A large box cage of about three to four feet in length, nearly two feet in width, and slightly more in height is suitable for most of the smaller owls and falcons. It may also be used for small hawks, but these are less suitable indoors because their droppings are ejected with some force for several hours after they have fed, and the cage and its surroundings are difficult to keep clean.

The floor of the cage should be covered by a metal tray which slides out for cleaning. It may be scrubbed off every day or covered with peat or even paper (although some birds have the habit of tearing paper); on no account should sand be used. Two perches should be provided, one at each side of the cage and far enough in for the bird's tail to miss the sides if it leans forward. The perches should be thick, about the span of the bird's toes in diameter. A small wooden block and a dish of water may also be provided. Wire mesh should not be used for the front of the cage; a wire frame with as few horizontal bars as possible, or thin wooden slats will lessen damage to the bird's feathers. The door – ideally about nine inches high and seven wide – should be at the centre. A tame bird can then leave or enter the cage, provided that it has not just been fed, that highly polished surfaces have been covered to protect them from claws, breakable ornaments have been put away, and the windows closed!

A garden shed makes suitable accommodation for most medium to fairly large birds of prey and for any large owl. Seven feet by five feet is a useful size, but a large eagle owl or medium-sized eagle requires a little more space. The furniture should be the same as that in the box cage and the floor should consist of peat or clean soil. There should be one large wire window facing approximately south, and small ventilators at the ends which may be opened in hot weather. Small trees should be sited to give shade.

In general, birds should not be mixed together. If it is desired to keep two or more in a large shed, a device known as a screen perch is run the length of the shed. Each bird is tied to the screen perch by the leash attached to its jesses, at about four or five feet intervals. With some species, pairs may be kept loose in a shed together and sometimes a small group of mixed species (usually insectivorous or carrion-eating kinds) may agree together. Most kites, the majority of buzzards and vultures, and some of the smaller eagles are species which will usually live together. Hawks, most falcons (including kestrels) and most large eagles are generally best kept alone, otherwise they are likely to fight and may even kill one another.

Owls usually do well in pairs, but it is unwise to try trios except in the case of scops owls. The training of owls differs in that they are handled in bright artificial light, which tends to make them drowsy. But once tame, they are more inclined to fly for food in dull evening light. They are also more inclined to breed in captivity than are birds of prey. But even so considerable difficulties are involved and a large quantity of natural food (mice, small birds, and so on) is required for both adults prior to breeding and for the young.

Raw, lean beef usually forms the basic diet for raptorial birds in captivity. The approximate amount required for birds of different sizes is given on Page 23. Meat should be cut into small strips for the smaller insectivorous species and into long strips for snake eaters. Most of the large, strong-footed species may be given beef bones to give their beaks and neck muscles exercise. Many species naturally eat fish, and meal worms and blow-fly larvae are given to small hawks and to owls. Entire animals, such as mice for small species, and rabbits for larger ones, are necessary at regular intervals to provide essential roughage, vitamins and minerals. This balanced diet is essential. Amounts of food given must be controlled carefully; too much is almost as harmful as too little, although an occasional gorge will do no harm. Birds should always show enthusiasm at their feeding time.

Most birds of prey enjoy being placed outside on their blocks or perches for a while each day when they can have a change of scenery. They appreciate both the rain and the sunshine and open their wings to receive the warm rays. Strong winds unsettle them and they must not be left out in really bad weather.

BOOKS TO READ

A Hawk for the Bush by J. G. Mavrogordato. H. F. and G. Witherby Ltd., London, 1960.

A Manual of Falconry by M. H. Woodford. Adam and Charles Black, London, 1960.

Birds of Prey by Philip Brown. Andre Deutsch, London, 1964.

Birds of Prey of the World by Mary L. Grossman and John Hamlet. Cassell, London, 1965.

Birds of the British Isles Volumes 4 and 5 by David A. Bannerman and George E. Lodge. Oliver and Boyd, Edinburgh and London, 1956.

Eagles by Leslie Brown. Michael Joseph, London, 1955.

Eagles, Hawks and Falcons by Leslie Brown and Dean Amadon. Country Life, London and McGraw-Hill, New York, 1969.

Handbook of British Birds Volumes 2 and 3 by H. F. Witherby et al. H. F. and G. Witherby Ltd., 1947.

Life Histories of North American Birds of Prey Volumes 1 and 2 by A. C. Bent. Dover Publications Inc., New York, 1961.

Pirates and Predators by R. Meinerzhagen. Oliver and Boyd, London and Edinburgh, 1959.

The Art and Practice of Hawking by E. B. Michell. Holland Press Ltd., London, 1959.

The Buzzard by Frank Wenzel. Allen and Unwin, London, 1959.

The Golden Eagle King of Birds by Seton Gordon. Collins, London, 1955.

PLACES TO VISIT

London Zoo (Zoological Society of London), Regents Park, London, N.W.1. About 50 different species of diurnal birds of prey and 25 species of owls are on view.

Welsh Mountain Zoo, Colwyn Bay, Denbighshire.
  A zoo specializing in birds of prey and owls.

Twycross Zoo, Nr. Atherstone, Warwickshire.
  A good collection of birds of prey and owls.

The following zoos also have good birds of prey and owl collections: Chester Zoo   Bristol Zoo.

The following zoos generally show a number of birds of prey and owls: Paignton Zoo   Colchester Zoo.

The Norfolk Wildlife Park, Great Witchingham, Norfolk.

Edinburgh Zoo.

The Falconry Centre, Newent, Gloucestershire.

There is a fine bird gallery at the British Museum (Natural History), Cromwell Road, London, S.W.7 but the research collection is now housed at The Museum, Tring, Hertfordshire.

SOME OTHER TITLES IN THIS SERIES

Hamlyn all-colour paperbacks

Birds of Prey

Glenys and Derek Lloyd

illustrated by Ken Lilly

Hamlyn
London · New York · Sydney · Toronto

FOREWORD

Since early civilisation men have been fascinated by the hunters of the air – the birds of prey and owls. They appear in some of the early works of art, and some forms were trained for hunting over 4,000 years ago.

Today they are in decline in many parts of the world through the destruction of their natural habitat, poisoning by toxic chemicals, and human persecution, which is a tragedy as apart from their aesthetic appeal these birds are valuable to man because most of their prey consists of animals which compete with us for food.

This authoritative book lists all the birds of prey and owls existing in the world today, with brief details of the hunting and nesting of the better known and more spectacular kinds. The common and scientific names, comparative size and geographical range of all species are given, and accurate colour illustrations depict many of them.

Most aspects of the life histories of these birds are discussed in other chapters of this book, and a final chapter describes management in confinement and gives a brief review of falconry with the birds most often used in this sport.

Throughout this book we have endeavoured to keep scientific and falconry terms to a minimum as it is intended primarily for the layman with an interest in birds. However, the serious ornithologist may also find it useful as some chapters – such as those on food requirements, and the reasons for size differences between the sexes in some species – contain original work and discuss new ideas.

Finally, with regard to the last section, we should like to point out that under the 1954–67 Protection of Birds Acts it is illegal to take and keep any British bird of prey or owl without a licence from the Home Office. It is also now illegal to import any bird of prey or owl into Britain unless under licence.

G. and D. L.

Published by The Hamlyn Publishing Group Limited
London · New York · Sydney · Toronto
Astronaut House, Feltham, Middlesex, England

Copyright © The Hamlyn Publishing Group Limited 1969
Reprinted 1971, 1972, 1974, 1975, 1976
ISBN 0 600 00101 6

Phototypeset by Jolly & Barber Limited, Rugby, Warwickshire
Colour separations by Schwitter Limited, Zurich
Printed in Spain by Mateu Cromo, Madrid